Secrets for Getting Things Done

Strategies to Take Your Productivity to the Next Level

To DearFriend,

Best to You!

Vince Harris

Secrets for Getting Things Done:
Strategies to Take Your Productivity to the Next Level

Published by
Beckworth Publications
3108 E. 10th St.
Trenton, Mo 64683

ISBN: 978-0-9847952-6-0

Library of Congress Cataloging-in-Publication Data
Harris, Vincent

Secrets for Getting Things Done:
Strategies to Take Your Productivity to the Next Level
by Vincent Harris

Library of Congress Control Number: 2014903167

Typeset in 11pt Gentium Basic by Amanda MacCabe

Printed in the United States of America

Contents

Introduction   ix

Strategy #1:
Plan the Night Before   1

Strategy #2:
Use the 80/20 Rule   5

Strategy #3:
The Law of Forced Efficiency   10

Strategy #4:
See the Task as Already Being Done   13

Strategy #5:
Fill Out a Time Log   18

Strategy #6:
Know the Truth About Expectations   23

Strategy #7:
Learn to Play the "How Much Can I Do" Game   27

Strategy #8:
Get Up An Hour Before You Have To   30

Strategy #9:
De-clutter   33

Strategy #10:
90-Day Rule for Creating Change
Resistant Habits   36

Strategy #11:
Create a Stress and Worry Chair   40

Strategy #12:
Be a Note Sender and a Gift Giver   44

Strategy #13:
Review Your Day Each Evening   50

Strategy #14:
Do at Least One Thing Each Day Out of Your Comfort Zone   55

Strategy #15:
Adopt the "If I'm on Time, I'm Late" Philosophy   62

Strategy #16:
Box Yourself in For Success   68

Contents

Strategy #17:
Your Mind Will Process Faster Than You Think 72

Strategy #18:
Get Rid of All But Three of Your Email Folders 77

Strategy #19:
Learn to Say "No" 83

Strategy #20:
Eat a Light Lunch 91

Strategy #21:
Estimate the Time and Add 50 % 96

Strategy #22:
Let People Know Upfront How Much Time You Have 99

Strategy #23:
Don't Live by Assumptions; Operate on Facts 103

Strategy #24:
The Mouse Exercise 112

Strategy #25:
Why Affirmations Rarely Work 115

About the Author 125

Introduction

In this book I'm going to share nearly 25 different strategies and concepts that will allow you to get more of the important things done in life and radically increase your productivity while simultaneously boosting your energy, so you can really squeeze the juice out of the experience of life and get more happiness and inner peace along every step of your journey through life.

My personal library is replete with books, videos, DVDs, and audio programs, and that all started with my first copy of Think and Grow Rich, in 1978. For many years now, I have believed, as speaking icon Jim Rohn often talked about, that the person that does not read is no better off than the person who cannot. So, congratulations; you are taking an active role in your life by continually learning new things and exposing yourself to new ideas.

In this book, *The Secrets for Getting Things Done*, you'll find solutions. In the pages that follow, I'm going to offer you a series of invitations. Each strategy, tool, or technique I share with you will be an opportunity for you to embrace something new and useful. Now, do I think that you'll embrace every idea? It's highly unlikely. I suspect that you're far too unique as a human being for a cookie-cutter approach to work for you. That's exactly why I'm sharing so many different strategies with you in this book, so you can pick and choose, intelligently sculpting a highly customized system to move forward at a rapid pace.

I should tell you this; you will see some things that aren't necessarily standard, or what your English professor would see as "appropriate" in the coming pages. There is a reason for anything like this you might notice. This book was written to impart, to you, the strategies for getting things done, and to do so at the deepest neurological level of processing possible. You'll see numbers as "3", instead of "three" like you might see in other books, or as your English professor or teacher might have demanded. Why? Because when you are reading, your brain processes "3" for example, much differently that it processes "three", and it is in this difference in processing what you are reading that deeper and more meaningful learning is taking place. That is my utmost concern, for you, and not that I would get a good mark if my chapter was submitted to be graded.

You'll find other things, as well, but I'll leave them for you to discover, as you are enjoying the process of also discovering strategies that will allow you to get more accomplished in life.

Strategy #1:

Plan the Night Before

"By failing to prepare, you are preparing to fail"
-BENJAMIN FRANKLIN

In the 1920s, a gentleman by the name of Ivy Lee walked into the offices of Charles Schwab and made a pretty outlandish claim. He said, "Mr. Schwab, if you will give me 15 minutes with each of your managers, I will radically transform productivity around here."

Now Schwab was no dummy, and frankly, that sounded like a whole lot of gibberish. However, Lee then came back with an offer that made it irresistible. He said, "Mr. Schwab, if you will give me 15 minutes with each of your managers, all I ask is that in 90 days, you just write out a check for what it's been worth to you."

This, of course, was enticing to Schwab; it was an offer he just couldn't turn down. Ivy Lee didn't spend 15 minutes with each of those managers. Ivy Lee spent about 10 minutes with each of the managers, and 90 days later, Charles Schwab sat down at his desk and wrote out a check for the equivalent of today's money, of $600,000.

$600,000 and all Ivy Lee did was spend about 10 minutes with each of the managers. Are you curious about what he told them? I forewarn you, it's so simple and so easy to do that there's a tendency, initially, to say, "Oh, that? I can do THAT!" If that's the thought that comes to your mind when I reveal it to you in a moment, then I ask you to consider this question: If you know about it, have you been doing it consistently?

Here it is: Ivy Lee said to each of those managers, "The night before, write down the number 1 through six on a piece of paper, and then write down the 6 most important things you have to do the next day." Here's the key difference between the list Ivy Lee was suggesting and any other list: You only write down the 6 most important things you have to do the next day as they relate to your overall goal or mission for that week.

You can probably already see that this is wildly different from the average list that you might have made in the past because a lot of the time, people just scrawl down anything that pops into their head, and they are not measuring it or contrasting it against anything of importance. They're just writing down what comes to mind, which is generally the most pressing or most urgent things, and as you'll find out later, this can lead to trouble.

Another mistake that people often make when creating a list is writing down more than 6 things. Sometimes people in a workshop or a seminar raise their hand and tell me, "Vince, I use a list already and it really doesn't work." Invariably, when I ask them, "How many things are on your typical list?" I'll get answers of 12, 15, or as high as 20. This creates chaos.

The reason things are overwhelming at 12, 15, or 20 is something that a man by the name of George Miller examined in the

1960's. Miller wrote a paper called "Seven Plus/Minus Two" and it described what Miller had discovered about human consciousness and our ability to only hold 5 to 9 chunks of information in our awareness at any given time. Beyond that, we go into overwhelm, get confused, and things can get mixed up pretty quickly. You can see where a list of 12, 15, or 20 things, then, is actually working against us when it comes to increasing our productivity.

So, before we move on, remember, Ivy Lee said to write down the numbers 1 through 6, and then write down the 6 most important things you have to do the next day *as they related to your overall goal or mission for the week.*

Before you write something down, you're looking forward at the next 5 to 7 days, and asking: for the primary outcome that I have for this week, what's the first important thing that relates to this goal, this project, or this outcome? Only then does it go down, if indeed, it is important as it relates to your desired outcome.

Now, here comes the really hard part of what Ivy Lee told the managers of Charles Schwab. He said, "As you do them the next day, cross them off. Those that you don't get that day, go to the top of the next day's list". Let me ask you this; have you ever written something you needed to do down on a list and you didn't get to it, and you didn't carry it forward to the next day's list?

If so, what happens next is predictable, is it not? Does the phrase "out of sight, out of mind" ring a bell? Ivy Lee knew something important about human consciousness. Once something was not in front of us anymore, we wouldn't be thinking about it. Lee's answer to that challenge was to simply bring it forward to the next day's list.

Have you ever made a list, and just when you were about to finish your list, you thought of something that you had already done that morning? Something that you had forgotten about having already done, and then you go ahead and write it on your list so you can have the pleasure of crossing it off? I know I am guilty of this. That should tell you how much we like to cross things off of a list, and how much we like to feel good about what we've done. Ivy Lee knew this as well, and he knew that if he could get people to cross things off as they completed them, that they would be linking good feelings to getting things done. Each time they marked off a task they had just finished, they would literally be anchoring those powerful and useful feelings to having completed the task.

To say that the Ivy Lee method of creating a list has made a difference in my life would be an understatement. I can say with certainty, that getting my first book written was something that probably would not have happened were it not for my daily use of thinking about and writing down the 6 most important things I had to do, the night before. It's simple, it's powerful, and it works.

Strategy #2:

Use the 80/20 Rule

"There are 10 golden rules for successful careers in an increasingly 80/20 world. The winners in any field have, almost by definition, found ways to make 20 percent of effort yield 80 percent of the results"
-RICHARD KOCH

Many years ago, an Italian economist by the name of Vilfredo Pareto discovered something that is the equivalent of rocket fuel when it comes to your ability to increase your productivity. Pareto looked at his country and found that 80% of the wealth was owned by just 20% of the people. This fascinated him, and as he began to look at other areas of life, he found this 80/20 ratio just about everywhere he looked. I'm confident that if you'll examine your own life or your productivity, you will find it too.

For example, in most any organization, 80% of the sales will come from just 20% of the salespeople. Out of every 100 salespeople in any given company, a mere 20 people will be selling more than 3/4 of all of the products or services that are sold each month. The other 80 people, combined, will sell only 20%

of everything that is sold in a given month. If you look at any stock portfolio, you'll find that about 80% of the worth of that stock portfolio comes from 20% of the stocks in that portfolio, and 80% of the stocks in that portfolio will account for only 20% of its worth. 80% of the thefts in a store are done by 20% of the shoplifters, and the other 20% is done by the other 80% of shoplifters. 80% of the cookies sold by a Girl Scout Troop will be sold by just 20% of the Girl Scouts, with the other 20% of cookies sold being sold by the other 80%. Almost everywhere you are willing to look, if you examine closely you'll find the 80/20 rule alive and well.

What if you were to examine your own life and discover that 80% of the results that you create come from just 20% of the things that you do? Would it be a good guess that you would probably focus more on doing the 20% of the things that are creating 80% of the results that you get?

That's exactly what you want to do. Conversely, what if you saw that 80% of the actions you were taking each day were only contributing to 20% of the results you were getting? Would you stop doing some of those things, realizing that in the grand scheme of things, many of those actions were close to being a waste of time?

The problem for most people is that they have no idea what actions or behaviors they are doing are truly making a difference, and which are not. They don't know what 8 actions out of 10 are only leading to 20% of their results, and which 2 out of 10 are leading to a whopping 80% of their results.

The best way that I have found to work with this is to write down a list of all of the things you have to do for a project. For example, let's say that you've got a project and you write down everything that's going to have to be done to complete that project. Let's say you come up with 100 actions. Whatever it is that you come up with, divide that number by 5. In this case, if you had 100 items listed, and you divided that number by five, you would come up with 20 things. 20 actions, 20 behaviors, and twenty things to do out of that 100. This is your 80/20 number. So, 100 divided by 5 gives you 20. That means, you're going to go through that list of 100 with a fine-tooth comb, and you're going to look for the 20 things out of 100 that will lead to 80% of the results that project's going to create.

You can do this with most anything. I just used 100 for an example because it's an easy number to work with. If you had ten things on a list and you divide that by 5, you come up with two. That means, out of a list of 10 actions that you need 2 actions, 10 behaviors that you're engaging in. When you take that number of things you are looking at and divide it by 5, you're going to narrow it down to the answer you get. In this case, using the example of 100, it is 10. You had 10 actions you needed to complete. Only 2 of those actions, just 2, will contribute to 80% of the results of that entire list.

When you have used this on just one project or goal you have that you want to get done, you'll know in your gut, just how effective this is, and how much of a difference it makes, because you will have applied the 80/20 Rule and reaped the tremendous rewards that it yields. In short, you will have gotten feedback that says "YES! This works so well that I can't imagine how I ever made it without this!"

Once you have done that, things get so much easier because

then you're beginning to look at our list of the projects that you have to do and you're beginning to see them with the eye of a surgeon. You're beginning to look for details you weren't looking for before, and what you'll find is a lot of those things that you were doing in the past that you thought were so important that you'd allow to stress you out, you're now willing to comfortably slide to the back burner because you know where they rank in terms of importance.

Now, let me clear one thing up now. It doesn't mean that the things you slide to the back burner won't have to be done at all, although that will be the case in time. It just means that if you are going to get the most accomplished possible, and wind up not being able to do everything, the things you don't get to will be the least important in terms of their contribution to the results that are important. It also means once you've defined and identified the most important 20% of those actions, behaviors, techniques, that's where you're going to allow yourself to focus.

Since repetition is the mother of learning, I want to look, once again, at the side of this equation that most people who talk about the 80/20 Rule ignore. It's absolutely crucial to keep in mind that if it's true that 20% of the actions and behaviors account for 80% of the results, then it's also true that 80% of the actions and behaviors only contribute to 20% of the results you will get.

This, I might add, is where the people who are always struggling, really working hard but always struggling in terms of they're just not producing and not achieving their goals, get hung up; it's generally because they have this 80/20 rule backward. They are caught up in working diligently and furiously on the 80% of the things that only contribute to 20% of the results.

Focus on the 20% that gets almost everything...and your life will change.

Strategy #3:

The Law of Forced Efficiency

"The trouble with lying and deceiving is that their deficiency depends entirely upon a clear notion of the truth that the liar and deceiver wishes to hide"

-HANNAH ARENDT

Have you ever felt the pressure of having a lot to do, thinking that you won't have time to do everything, but then telling yourself, "I HAVE to get it ALL done!!"? Most people have experienced this numerous times, with some people experiencing it several times a week. The only solution they can fathom is to just get everything done...to finish EVERYTHING. With only one solution on their radar, the loop of stress continues.

The only way out of a loop, is to get out of the loop. If you are on a roller coaster that does nothing but one BIG loop, over and over again, and at some point you decide you have had enough of looping, nothing you do will change your experience short of getting out of the loop. In this case, that means getting off of the ride.

The way to get out of the loop of stress that comes from persistent thoughts of, "I HAVE to get it ALL done!!" is to apply The Law of Forced Efficiency. What is The Law of Forced Efficiency?

The Law of Forced Efficiency states:

There will never be enough time to do *everything*. BUT, there will always be enough time to do the *most important thing*.

Let me ask you, what would happen if you got your "to do" list done right now? Would you be completely at ease and at peace and kick your feet up and lay in a hammock? You might think you would, but in reality, that's not usually what happens.

Your mind would immediately begin filling in and creating another list, and there's an unlimited number of things in the back of your mind that you could always be doing. So, the first part of The Law of Forced Efficiency is highly accurate when it says, "there will never be enough time for everything."

Yet, isn't it also true that a great deal of the stress we experience in life comes from this usually unconscious belief or unconscious concept that we hold in our mind that says, "if you're really a 'go getter' or a really productive human being, you'll get everything done"?

If that's the guideline that we're using, we're going to be in trouble. That belief will lead to inevitable agony and decreased motivation when we see that we might not be able to get everything done.

Let's look at the second part of The Law of Forced Efficiency. There will always be enough time for the most important thing. If that's the case, it becomes paramount then that we are able to determine, each day, each week, each month, each quarter, what the most important activities happen to be.

To be able to look at and determine, what's the most important thing right now or what the most important thing today is, or the most important thing this week; THIS is where we will find that "magic" when it comes to increasing our productivity using this strategy.

I think you'll find there will always be enough time for whatever it is that you have determined is most important for today. There will always be enough time for that. Just let a nice, easy feeling settle in on you when you finally accept that there won't always be enough time for everything, and decide that you're going to become a detective of finding the most important things each day.

By becoming a modern day Sherlock Holmes, waking up each day to find those otherwise elusive "most important" actions, you'll find yourself wanting to play more and more, and when you do, you get better at playing, and your ability to increase your productivity virtually explodes to a new level.

Strategy #4:

See the Task as Already Being Done

"I believe that visualization is one of the most powerful means of achieving personal goals"
-HARVEY MACKAY

This is one of my favorite strategies, and I've utilized this with countless clients from all over the world over the last 15 years. I've used it to assist them in doing everything from losing weight to improving their finances. I discovered early on that one of the major differences between people who tend to procrastinate and put important things off, and those who didn't procrastinate the important things and just got them done, was what was going on inside their head in terms of *how they were thinking* about what it was they needed to do.

For example, let's look at someone who always has a sink full of dirty dishes. They may always say or think, "Tonight, I'm not letting them just sit there. I'm going to get them done!" However, they get up the next morning to a sink full of dirty dishes from the night before. If you do something like this, you might wonder "Why do I do that?"

The real question, however, is, "*How* do I do that?" "Why?" usually invites excuses, and we come up with all kinds of reasons that make us feel more justified in continuing the behavior. "How?", though, looks at what we do in terms of our thinking, and once we know the answer to this, we also have a good idea what we can STOP doing, that will interrupt the negative pattern. So, again the most useful question is "How do I do this?"

The answer to the "How do I do this?" question is rather simple. People who procrastinate think of the sink full of dirty dishes, and then get a bad feeling about the drudgery involved in dealing with those dirty dishes. Then, they MOVE AWAY from the whole thing, by doing anything OTHER than the dishes. People who rarely procrastinate think about the dishes being done and the sink being empty, and then get a good feeling about having an empty sink and clean dishes put away. Then, they MOVE TOWARDS doing the dishes. They are chasing that good feeling, focusing on it, all the way through to the end, feeling better and better with each dish that is washed because it's one dish closer to the good feeling associated with having the empty sink.

So, let's look at this again.

For the person who procrastinates, the thought is: "I *should* do the dishes."

They create a thought or make a mental picture of the sink being full of dirty dishes. This, thought or inner image, triggers and generates a "bad" feeling about that image, and then it's just a natural consequence to move away from the bad feeling. In this case, what's the easiest way they can move away from the bad feeling? By procrastinating. Isn't it the true that the moment you procrastinate something, you get a sense of relief?

Oftentimes, in my workshops and my seminars I'll say, "Can I see the number of hands in here of people who, no matter what, always have your dishes done and they're never sitting in the sink or they're never piled up next to the sink. You just wash them, get them done, and put away immediately?" Invariably, a few hands will go up.

At that point, I'll ask them to track along with me because what I'm going to do is explain to the others who didn't raise their hands, what I have found to be true of most people who rarely procrastinate, and I want them to weigh it against their personal experience and see if they agree with me.

I say, "The person who has the thought "I should do the dishes", and actually gets them done, makes a picture in their mind of the dishes already being done; already being washed and completely put away, and then they get a good, or a positive feeling about that internal image.

Human beings do everything they do to accomplish one of two things. Any given action is either taken to move away from pain, or towards pleasure.

Now, in the first example, the person was procrastinating. They were presenting themselves with an image that they wanted to move away from, and in doing so, they procrastinated in doing the dishes. The person in the second example presents themselves with an image that feels good. It's an image that they want to move towards. The only way they can hold on to that feeling, the only way they can achieve that feeling, in their mind, is by making their external reality match with their internal reality that they are experiencing.

Now, it's also interesting to note that they have this good feeling *while* they are engaged in the process of *doing* the dishes.

So, rather than it being something that they only get to experience when the dishes are done, because of the way they set things up in their mind, they get to have the good feeling just because they're presenting themselves with an image of the dishes already being done. They get to hold on to that feeling while they're doing the dishes, and when the dishes are actually done and put away, it just seals the deal, so to speak.

It's a positive loop. Every time they think about doing the dishes, they will feel good. Every time they actually do the dishes, they feel good. When they get them done, they feel good, and so it's a self-perpetuating loop.

The person who is procrastinating doing all the dishes all the time, they're in this loop as well, but it's a self-perpetuating negative loop. They think about doing the dishes, they feel bad. They push away from doing the dishes, and they feel bad about that. They now have more dishes to do, and so now the picture in their minds is of more dishes so they feel even worse about that and they move away from that even faster, and on and on it goes.

What else could you do this with? Anything that you might have, in the past, procrastinated.

People often have good intentions and maybe their doctor has told them, "You really need to start exercising because you've got diabetes and heart disease on both sides of the family." That makes logical sense to them, but then they don't follow through with their logic. They might take their shoes to work and a towel or their gym bag. They might plan for it in the morning. But then what happens next is fairly predictable.

Rather than making an image in their mind of seeing themselves already having walked, already having gone to the track and completed their 1-mile, 2-mile, or 3-mile run, and then feeling good about that image, the the image they create in their mind is of seeing themselves huffing and puffing and straining as they run, or as they walk, and their legs ache, and they see every step of the process, having to sit down and put their shoes on, and you know, of course, you have to take your other shoes off first. There are so many things to do. Is it any wonder they don't exercise?

They focus on the process and feel bad about it, and therefore, the only way they can get a sense of relief is to procrastinate...to NOT exercise; to move away from it, not do it, and they get this temporary sense of relief. But then what happens an hour or two later? That's right. The guilt kicks in. Now, they feel bad about not exercising.

See the task as already done, whatever it is, whether you want to exercise, whether you want to get the dishes done, whether you want to get your taxes done, or whether you want to practice for the upcoming presentation. Whatever it is, in your mind see the task as already having been done and completed.

Feel good about that image and you'll set up this internal system that wants to move towards DOING something.

Strategy #5:

Fill Out a Time Log

"There are far too many people who waste their time telling themselves that they don't have enough time"
-DANIEL WILEY

Let's talk about a time log. Most people that I talk to, especially when they first meet with me, whether it be on a consultation or during a seminar, maybe during a break at a seminar, tell me how stressed out they are and how little time they have—that they have so much to do and not nearly enough time to do it.

One of the things I point out to them is that it very rarely comes down to not having enough time. It comes down to not knowing enough about the things we have to do, and which of the things we have to do are most important.

Very often, people balk at that and they say, "No, you don't understand, Vince. I really just don't have enough time. Every minute, every second of my day is jam packed. I couldn't squeeze any more in if I wanted to."

Let me tell you about the results of an anonymous survey

given to executives, asking them, "How much of each of your work days are productive hours? How much time is dedicated to producing a tangible and measurable result?" Do you think the answer these executives gave was 8 hours? How about 7? How about 6? 5? 4? 3? 1 hour?

What was the average of the executives that were surveyed and asked, "How many hours of your day are productive hours going into a measurable and tangible result?"? The answer was 1 hour per day. Yes, a single hour per day

Sometimes people kind of chuckle or laugh when I say this, and while it is kind of humorous, I'm serious as can be. If I were to walk into your office or workplace right now, look you in the eyes, and tell you that if you were to spend 3 hours with me, I would help you double your productivity, chances are, you would laugh and roll your eyes. Why? Because most of us think that the work it would take to double our productivity would be massive.

Do you know anybody right now, whether you know them personally or just know of them, who is making 3 to, perhaps, 4 times as much money as you are? I'm guessing the answer is yes, and if that's the case, I also want to ask you another question.

Do you think those people are working 3 to 4 times as many hours as you are? Do you think they are working 4 to 5 times harder than you are? The answer is obvious to both of those: of course not.

They could not be working 3 to 4 times longer than you are and they certainly aren't working 3 or 4 times harder. If, in fact, there are so many people in the world making 3 or 4 times more money than you, then what's going on?

When we come back to this time log, this is where we get an accurate picture of how we are using the time that we have each day. If you ask the average person who works an 8 hour workday, "how many hours are you working each day?" They'll say "8. I work 8 hours a day." If you press them a little bit and you say, "I know you have to be there 8 hours a day, but how many of those hours are you really working?" They might say, "I suppose maybe 6, or 6 1/2" The answer is probably wrong again.

When you fill out a time log, it means at the top of each hour- like 10:00 am- you write down the things that you've accomplished in the last hour, about how long they took you, and then at the end of the day, tally those things up and the time that they took. Sometimes you're astonished to find that, "Wow, I was here 8 hours, I was here 10 hours, I was here 12 hours, but when I tally up the time and look at how many of those hours were productive, it only comes to 5 hours, 4 hours, or maybe only 3 hours."

This is what you have to do to pierce that armor that we've all built around us that says, "I work hard!"

It's in this discretionary time we discover-the available time that we have not been using to be productive- that the real magic and transformation can occur. However, if you just fill out your time log for 1 day, it's not going to be the most accurate reflection of how you use your time.

Why? Because some days are more stressful than others, and some days are more relaxing. If you'll do a time log every day for a week, you'll get an average of how much free time, or discretionary time, you have available.

Feel free to extend this into your personal life and into your evening hours, because all too often, parents have told me that when they've gone home, they're convinced that they just don't have enough time to get everything done that they need to do that evening with their kids.

First, find out how much discretionary time you really do have available. Then, find out how much of that time in the evening you've been frittering away on useless activities that could have been devoted to your children, spouse, or some type of personal development. I dare you to conduct this time log experiment. I would love to hear from you. If you do the time log, and of 8 hours at work, it comes out that you are actually working 8 hours, I'd love to hear from you—the exception. I'd also love to hear from you after you do the time log and you find that out of 8 hours, you are actually only doing something productive 4 of those hours.

Let's come back to the executives that were surveyed. Only 1 hour of their workday was productive. Remember, I said, if I came into your office and said "I will help you double your productivity," I thought you would be very skeptical about that because it seems like this overwhelming, daunting task, doesn't it?

Yet, if we go back to these executives who were getting 1 hour of productive time in a day, do you realize that to double their productivity, it would only require them to move from 1 hour of productive time a day, to 2 hours a day?

You can do the same. If you discover that you only have 3 hours of productive time a day, and you move that from 3 to 6, you have now doubled your productivity, and I've worked with people who have tripled their productivity. I don't think I have to tell you how much that equates to in terms of financial gains, not to mention the other benefits. Do it, enjoy it...love it.

Strategy #6:

Know the Truth
About Expectations

*"There were two ways to be happy: improve your reality,
or lower your expectations"*
—JODI PICOULT

A favorite quote of mine, from Dr. Michael L. Hall, is this: "We do not rise to the level of our expectations: we fall to the level of our training."

Let's take a look at this and see how this might be best applied for getting more things done. A lot has been written about the power of expectations, much of it being useful. A lot of my feedback from those that I've closely worked with over the years, shows that if you expect to succeed, you're likely to do and engage in activities that will lead to the success you seek. However, when we look at our expectations as the vehicle that will carry us from point A to point B, we often set ourselves up for trouble.

If we go back to the quote, "We do not rise to the level of our expectations; we fall to the level of our training." What does that mean? Let's say, for example, that you're working in a position that you're just not terribly crazy about. You'd like to do something else. You can do this until you get to the point when you can transition into something else, but you've really got your sights set on becoming a professional speaker.

If we look at what a lot of books have written about expectations, we can say, "Well, you know, I will just expect to become a professional speaker. I'll think about it and I will dwell upon it and I will write down affirmations.

I mean, I will expect, with every fiber of my being, to become a professional speaker."

Yet, if you're not reading about the kinds of things you need to read about and need to know to become a professional speaker, if you're not doing those things that you're reading about, and if you're not going out and actually giving presentations and giving free speeches to your local organizations such as the Lion's Club, the Kiwanis, or the Rotary Club...if you're not actually practicing those skills, then all of the expectation in the world may make you feel good about becoming a professional speaker, but it's not going to translate into you ever *becoming* a professional speaker.

It's a situation where you can expect all you want, but if you never *do* any of the things we can fit into the category of training, chances are, you're not going to become a professional speaker, or if you do, you probably won't be a very good one.

Let's turn that around. Let's say you are reading books on professional speaking, communication, or body language, and you are going out and speaking on a topic you are passionate about to organizations in your local community. You're actually getting up in front of people and you're honing your craft. You're practicing those skills that you're listening to on audio programs and reading about. In other words, you are training. In this scenario, it really doesn't matter if your level of expectation was a little lower than the previous example. What's ultimately going to happen is you're going to fall to your level of training. If your level of training is where it should be or beyond, then that's a pretty good place to fall to.

Let's look at a S.W.A.T. team. What if the S.W.A.T. team leader said to the team members, "Let's sit around and focus on your expectations about being able to go in and adequately nullify this hostage situation." However, let's say they never went to the range to shoot or do target practice; they didn't do room clearing, or go into the mock-up houses where they come in through doorways and see bad guys and have things pop up; they never did push-ups or sit ups, went to the gym and lifted weights, or went out to run. In other words, they were in bad physical condition, but they had outstanding expectations about being able to do their job. Does that sound like a good plan?

Let me ask you, if you were the hostage in the situation that I'm talking about where this S.W.A.T. team was coming in to rescue you, how good would you feel knowing they hadn't been training? If you knew that they were physically out of shape and that they hadn't fired their weapons in 3 months, how good would you feel about knowing they were coming in to get you?

While you may prefer to never have to be a hostage, (so would I) if you wound up as a hostage, isn't it true that if you knew that they had been to the range 3 times a week for the last 9 months, fired thousands of rounds through their weapons, and that they'd been through the mock-up house- the buildings where they practice coming in through the door and taking out bad guys, and had done that countless hours, and all of them were in peak, physical shape for their age, isn't it true you'd feel better about that, even if their expectations were a little shaky?

Remember, ultimately, we will not rise to the level of our expectations; we fall to the level of our training.

Strategy #7:

Learn to Play the "How Much Can I Do" Game

"You can be childlike without being childish. A child always wants to have fun. Ask yourself, 'Am I having fun?'"

—CHRISTOPHER MELONI

The "How Much I Can Do" game is radically different from the game that most people play. Most people play this kind of game: If they're trying to break things down into smaller pieces, they say, "Okay. I'm going to write 5 pages on my book." Or, "I'm going to do 3 pages on my dissertation or thesis." In other words, they give themselves a predetermined amount of work that they're going to do before they'll allow themselves to stop.

What I'm proposing is that you play the "How Much Can I Do" game and that it uses time as the variable. For example, if you set your cell phone's alarm to go off in 15 minutes, rather than there being a predetermined amount in terms of pages you are going to write, you are now working against the clock. You are going to see how many pages you are going to get done in 15 minutes.

What happens is this. Let's say that you get 3 pages done in 15 minutes. Tomorrow, or later this afternoon, or whenever you play the "How Much Can I Do" game again, here's what's going to happen. The 3 pages are going to serve as the benchmark of what you are able to get done in that 15 minutes time. It's going to become a game. You're going to find yourself just like a child, engaging in this, wondering, "can I beat my previous best?"

Rather than telling yourself, "I'm going to write 3 pages," or "I'm going to write 5 pages," which now seems like this burden, you've reversed the flow, so to speak. Now you're wanting to get 4 pages instead of 3 pages, or you're wanting to get 5 pages instead of 4 pages because you're working against time.

For reasons I really can't explain, I just know this works beautifully, and I've employed this with so many of my clients over the years. When you start working against the clock and your goal becomes to top your previous best, it becomes fun, and you want to do more. In fact, what you'll find is that sometimes the alarm will go off and you don't want to stop. You say, "Man, I don't want to stop now. I want to write another page."

Here's what I would urge you to do, at least initially, so you can really get this wired in so it works for you. If you decide to work for 15 minutes, when the alarm goes off, stop. Leave yourself with that feeling of wanting more. That's a good feeling to have. It's a very different feeling from the one you experienced in the past. In the past, you wanted so much to be able to stop earlier and not have to work for that extra 5 pages. You just wanted to be done.

If you're working against the clock, you'll find yourself wanting to do a little bit more or cheat a little bit and do 5 more minutes.

Remember, to get this wired in so that you're really locking in those psychological processes that allow this to really fuel you forward, whatever the time period is that you decide you're going to work, whether it be 5, 10, 15 minutes, stop whenever your alarm goes off. That's a wonderful feeling to have.

I can't tell you the joy I experienced the first time that I was out of time and I wanted to keep working past my alarm. When you begin to contrast that feeling with the previous feeling that you had of not even wanting to start, you'll find that very useful in terms of your productivity.

So it's real simple. You take a block of time, and in that block of time, you're going to get as much done as you can on whatever you're working on. When the alarm goes off, you're done. You can do this several times a day if you like.

Whatever it is, when the alarm clock goes off, you stop. Take some time to do something else such as take a walk to allow a gap between those segments of time. I think you'll find that this is something that creates this desire in you to start tackling these things that you've been putting off for so long.

There's a time limit. By noticing how much you can get done within that time limit, and then experiencing that innate human desire to do better than you did last time, you'll find your productivity going through the roof.

Strategy #8:

Get Up An Hour Before You Have To

"I wake up every morning and grab for the morning paper. Then I look at the obituary page. If my name is not on it, I get up"
— BENJAMIN FRANKLIN

I know that you might be thinking I'm crazy. "Get up an hour before I have to? Vince, when I get up now, I feel like I'm half dead and you want me to get up an hour before that?" Well clearly if you're going to do this intelligently, you can't go to bed at the time you currently are now and get up an hour before you have to.

My guess is that you're probably already shorting yourself on sleep. If you're tired when the alarm clock goes off and not ready to get out of bed, that's a pretty clear indication that you've not had enough sleep.

If you're currently going to bed at 11:00pm, and you start to get up an hour earlier than you do now, then that's 7 hours less sleep each week than you are getting now, and getting less is not going to be conducive to good health or productivity.

Clearly, this strategy of getting up an hour earlier would involve going to bed at least an hour earlier each evening so that you can, at the very least, have the same amount of sleep that you are currently getting and still be up an hour before you have to. But why get up an hour before you have to?

When you set your alarm clock for 6:00am the night before, you have determined that in order to have enough time to comfortably prepare for the day and not to have to rush around, you would need to be out of bed at 6:00am. When that alarm clock goes off at 6:00am, and you are now in a tired, sleepy frame of mind, you think: "Well, you know, if I slept another 10 or 15 minutes, and then just hurried when I did get up, I'd be okay."

As you know, hurry translates into stress and frustration, and when these two factors combine, it can lead to mistakes, forgetfulness, and just not getting the day off to a good start. Conversely, if you get up an hour before you have to, it starts the day with tranquility, and real peace that you can learn to count on each morning. It's a period of time when you can be up and do anything you want or choose to do, but a period of time when you don't *have* to do anything.

Remember, the more compressed the time span is, the more stressed you typically are. That's not a good way to start your day in terms of health, inner peace, and especially productivity.

By getting up an hour before you have to, you're able to engage your mind and you're able to start thinking about your day. You're also beginning to let the pieces from the night before-the things you planned-to fall into place.

I think of it as a comfortable running head start, where you haven't even started running yet. If you'll get up an hour before you have to for 1 week, the inner peace, tranquility, and the sense of calm that you experience just from doing this, is something that you'll learn to love, and this inner calm and inner peace you will experience will last the entire day.

Isn't it true that if your day starts off stressful, that it sometimes lasts the entire day? However, I think, somewhere in your past, you've had those days that started out really peaceful.

Maybe you just happened to wake up and get up earlier than you needed to, and there wasn't anything right then that you had to do. As you recall that now, you can remember how nice that was and how good it felt; and that feeling carried on into the morning and on into the afternoon. It made everything else that you did more efficient, more effective; you had a clearer head; you had more inner peace, and ultimately, your productivity went up.

Get up an hour earlier than you have to, and find out how many ways it benefits you!

Strategy #9:

De-clutter

---

*"Don't own so much clutter that you will be
relieved to see your house catch fire"*
-WENDELL BERRY

The idea of de-cluttering is not necessarily for the reason that you think. There are times when I say something about de-cluttering or organizing workspace, and people think it's just to make that work area more efficient so you're not bumping into something. While that's part of it, that's not my emphasis here. There tends to be a strong correlation between our external environment and what's going on internally.

If you were to walk into your office, or your bedroom, or your workspace that you use, right now, by looking at your external environment, you can get a really powerful snapshot of how organized your internal environment-your mind- is at any given time. A lot of people argue this, initially.

In other words, you can suggest this to somebody and they'll say, "I don't know if I believe that. I don't know if that's true. I believe I'm an organized and productive person, and my area is a mess, but I know where everything is." Have you ever heard that one before? I must confess, I have uttered that phrase before. While it may be true-that people may know where everything is-so does the person who has all of the pens in one drawer, all of the paper in a different drawer, and all of the paperclips in another drawer. They both "know where things are", however, they're also both reflecting what's going on internally.

There's no doubt about it, I have run into fairly productive people who had a desk that was an absolute mess. In every situation I've encountered this, if I could get that person to de-clutter, they went from being productive, to being ultra-productive. If you will extend this into your thinking and realize that anytime your thinking seems confused or cluttered, if it seems like you are just having a hard time sorting things out in your mind, the first place you might want to look is in your external environment.

It can often seem very difficult to get our internal world organized and de-cluttered. That's a little less tangible. That seems a little more difficult to do and yet, something anyone of us can do in a second's notice by just deciding; we can start to organize and de-clutter, and really straighten out our external world, and fortunately, we get a reciprocal effect when we do.

Stepping away from the internal world a little bit, focusing on lining up, de-cluttering and organizing the external world, and then stepping away from that for a little bit, we find that we bring the two into harmony and alignment.

It does work both ways. We can experience our external world collecting clutter because our internal world has become cluttered. However, we can also experience our internal world becoming cluttered because we've allowed our external world to become cluttered. Of the two, the one that's easier for most people, initially, to really get control of and to be able to do something about, is the external world.

De-clutter and organize by getting rid of the things you no longer use. Sometimes we look in a drawer and we say, "Well, I haven't used that for a while, but I could be using that soon." I have a rule that if I have not used something for 12 months, unless it's a family heirloom and has a whole lot of sentimental value, it goes out in the trash. Yes, sometimes I have a situation where I think to myself: "Man, I just threw that out because it surpassed the 12 month rule when maybe it would have been useful to have." More times than not, those things would have never been used again.

The thing is, as long as they are in the drawer, your closet, or anywhere in your environment and you're not using them, they are eating up mental space, simply by just being there. There's only so much room in consciousness for things to rest and wait to be used, in terms of thoughts, memories, projects, and planning.

Even if we're not thinking of those things, it can occupy space that can otherwise be used for something else. The bottom line is to de-clutter and get rid of things no longer needed or used. I know you'll enjoy what happens as a result.

Strategy #10:

90-Day Rule for Creating Change Resistant Habits

"The man who can't bear to share his habits is a man who needs to quit them"
-STEPHEN KING

One of the primary reasons people fail to increase their productivity, at least in the long haul, is they don't have the habits that will support increased productivity. Really, it's just as simple as that. You may remember a number of years ago when people talked about being able to establish a new habit in 21 days. I'll almost bet that you knew a whole lot of people who got excited about that and went out and did something for 21 days to create their new habit, but who are no longer doing that "new habit."

Today, we know, that resistant habits are not formed in 21 days; they're not even formed in 30 days. For a behavior to truly become a habit that's neurologically wired in, such that it becomes as easy to do as the old way of behaving, acting, or performing, it takes about 90 days.

This is pretty exciting because it pairs up with another challenge that people have. You see, so often times, people get excited that they're really going to increase their productivity, and that they're going to really get things done. They're going to go out and be a smashing success, and yet, it's not too long after they've embarked on this venture that they've changed their mind. They've quit because they've decided, "you know, that's just not for me."

Why does that happen? What happens to that excitement? Why do people "fall off the wagon," so to speak? Often times it comes down to this: They try to do too much at once. If you try to establish 6 new habits all at the same time, what's going to happen?

You get so overwhelmed because you have to consciously think about so many things that it just floods and overwhelms you. The only way to experience any relief from that is to eliminate 2 to 4 of them, or go back to your old way. The old way is familiar, and familiarity, as you know, is comfortable.

There are 4 quarters per year. Traditionally, we talk about that in business, but we also have 4 quarters a year in our personal lives. In fact, just in life in general, there are 4 quarters each year. Do you know someone who is light years ahead of you in terms of what you would call success? Someone a long way ahead of you in terms of finances, relationships, or in their career? Do you know somebody who is quite a bit ahead of you in some area of life, all because of a single habit they have that you don't have? Most people can very quickly say: "yes, absolutely. I know a lot of people that are WAY ahead of me, all because of a single habit they have that I don't have."

Let's take a look at finances because that is an area that is so measurable. Isn't it true that if you would have started investing

$100 a month in a mutual fund from the age of 18, you would have a significant chunk of money today? Most likely.

Is that a habit? Sure it is. Anything that you do repeatedly and consistently, and you've done since you were 18 years old (assuming you're 35 to 40 years old now) would certainly qualify as a habit. Does having a "good" habit for many years that someone else doesn't have, create a striking contrast between your condition and the condition of somebody that didn't develop that habit? Well, of course it does; and that's just a single habit.

So, clearly, a single habit can change someone's entire life. What if you developed 4 new habits a year? See, we have 4 quarters a year, approximately 3 months each, which, by the way, is 90 days. This just happens to coincide with how long it takes to develop a neurologically resistant habit.

It also allows you to avoid becoming overwhelmed by trying to do too much at once.

By using the 90 Day Rule for creating habits that are resistant to change, you're just going to pick a single new habit every 90 days. That's it; a single habit that you are going to work on establishing for the next 90 days. At the end of 90 days, you will pick another single habit, so that each year, at the end of each year, you will have 4 new habits.

We've already talked about how much of a difference 1 good habit you have that somebody else doesn't can make in your life. If you work on a new habit every 90 days, totaling 4 habits a year, then in 10 years, you have 40 new habits.

I remember, about 3 months ago, a lady in a seminar raised her hand and said, "Vince, in 10 years, I'll be 72 years old." I just kind of chuckled and smiled, and said, "Mary, how old will you be in 10 years if you don't develop 40 new habits?" She grinned, but then her grin vanished and a look of seriousness replaced it as she said, "You're absolutely right; I'll still be 72!"

Pick a single habit, work on it for 90 days, to really deeply get that habit to take root.. At the end of 90 days, that new habit will be as easy for you to do on a psychological and a neurological level as whatever it was you were doing before. That's not true after 21 days; after 21 days, you've kind of got a running head start, if you will, but if you stop for a few days, there's that old habit that's so much more comfortable and so much easier to do, because it is still more familiar.

That won't be the case after 90 days. In fact, after 90 days, if you were to try and go back to the old habit, which I don't suggest you do, but if you did, you would find that the old habit has now become the one that's feeling kind of strange and difficult. The new habit that you have formed in that 90 day period will be the one that feels comfortable and familiar.

Strategy #11:
Create a Stress and Worry Chair

"Worry does not empty tomorrow of its sorrow,
it empties today of its strength"
-CORRIE TEN BOOM

Now, you're probably thinking, "What? Create a Stress and Worry Chair? I'm looking for less stress and less worrying!" That's exactly the point. A lot of times in a seminar or a workshop that I'm doing, somebody will raise their hand and say, "Vince, have you got any tips, on how I might reduce the amount of stress in my life?" Usually they're somewhat taken aback when I give them the suggestion I will discuss, here.

So what's this about? Create a Stress and Worry Chair? I actually created this from a philosophy that Victor Frankl, the author of <u>Man's Search for Meaning</u>, talked about in his book. It's what he calls Paradoxical Intention. Paradoxical Intention came about when Frankl was working with his patients and found that he could jam up the mental or psychological processes that people utilized or unconsciously went through to create some of the symptoms that they were experiencing in their life that were troubling.

For example, he had a gentleman who came to him because every time he met someone new and would shake hands with them, the nervousness that he was experiencing would cause his palms to literally drip with sweat. You can imagine how embarrassing that might be for someone like a business contact, or perhaps a future wife or husband, and they extend their hand, only to have you with a cold, clammy, dripping wet hand, grasp theirs. Not a real good way to make a favorable first impression.

Frankl could only assume that anybody who had worked with this gentleman, had previously gone through the typical suggestions of relaxing and thinking kind thoughts; of having him think about floating clouds (or something like this) before he gets ready to meet somebody, in an attempt to get him to quit stressing and relax. You might be able to imagine what happened for this gentleman each time he tried to employ those tactics of relaxing. You guessed it; it only got worse. He got more nervous, making his hands sweat even more.

He was about at his wit's end. Frankl suggested to him, "Look, here's what I want you to do. First of all, will you do what I ask you to do as long as it will cause you no harm?" He said, "Sure, yeah. I'll do that as long as it's going to help and not going to cause me any harm, yeah, no matter how crazy it is, I'll do it."

Frankl said, "Well, then, here's what I want you to do. I want you to go out and introduce yourself to 8 or 10 people this week. However, I want you to do something different. Before you get ready to go meet each person and introduce yourself, I want you to spend a few moments getting yourself really nervous. I know you get nervous now. I know your hands get pretty wet and clammy now, but here's the task; I want you to get even more nervous;

I want your hands to sweat even more. I want you to make your hands perspire twice as much as they do now, if that's possible."

Now, that sounds pretty crazy at first, doesn't it? And yet, when this patient came back to see Frankl the following week, he was somewhat dejected, feeling he had failed this "experiment". Frankl inquired about what he had experienced. The patient's reply told the whole story. He said, "Dr. Frankl I don't know what I was doing wrong. I wasn't able to do that." He said, "I wasn't able to get myself any more nervous than before. I couldn't make my hands sweat any more than they had in the past. In fact, I couldn't get myself nervous at all. My hands were mysteriously dry and warm." This was exactly what Frankl had been striving for, which is why he asked him to make his symptoms even worse.

What does this have to do with a Stress and Worry Chair? Most people think there is really such a thing as "stress" in life. Interestingly, there is no such "thing" as stress. You can't find a "thing" called stress and put it in a bucket or a wheelbarrow. There are events that occur, and human beings that are *stressing*, in response to those events, but there is no such "thing" as stress. So, going back to the topic of the Stress and Worry Chair, let's examine how we can use a chair with paradoxical intention. Pick a particular chair in your house, or office, that will be used for nothing else other than going to sit in and worry.

This is important: You don't go to this chair *after* you've already started worrying or stressing. This chair will *only* be for sitting in to do nothing but stress and worry for a pre-determined time; you will go and sit in this chair and worry. That is the only purpose of that chair. All you are to do while sitting in that chair is to worry and engage in stressing as much as you can.

You'll find- just as the patients of Dr. Victor Frankl did when they employed these tools of paradoxical intention- that when you're trying to create the stressing, or when you're trying to worry or create the worrisome thoughts, you will find they just won't come. If they do start to come, you'll find they quickly flit away and tend to vaporize.

When you are using the Stress and Worry Chair, in the manner I have described, you will have reversed the psychological process; something that used to be an unconscious process, you've now turned it back into a conscious process, which jams up the psychological mechanisms that have allowed it to automatically and negatively influence your life in the past.

You'll start to see the futility of spending as much of your life as you had been, worrying and stressing. I might add, the only reason you had been spending that much time worrying and stressing, in the first place, was simply because it was an unconscious process. You really weren't conscious of how much time you were worrying and stressing, and you certainly weren't conscious in engaging in those processes.

That's the task. Write it down! Pick 5 to 10 minutes a day, go to your Stress and Worry Chair, and your task is to worry as hard as you can and to engage in stressing. I think you'll be surprised and delighted to discover what happens.

Strategy #12:

Be a Note Sender and a Gift Giver

"We make a living by what we get.
We make a life by what we give"

-WINSTON CHURCHILL

This one kind of speaks for itself, but let's talk about it and just explore a little further. Be a note sender and a gift giver. You probably remember when you were a child and you got a gift from somebody for your birthday or for Christmas, and maybe your grandmother or one of your parents said, "Sit down, I'd like for you to write them a thank you note." Whether you did it, or not, at least there was the awareness that it would probably be a good idea to send thank you notes.

For many people, there is this unspoken-but recognized-connection between the size or the magnitude of a gift they have received and the likelihood that they will sit down and write a thank you note to the person who gave them the gift. The "bigger" or more significant the gift, to the person who received it, the more likely they will send a thank you.

Let's say you're a guitar player, and somebody buys you a

$900 dollar guitar that they know you've been wanting, it's going to be a pretty significant gift to you.

Most people wouldn't find it difficult to sit down and write a thank you note for the gift of the guitar, in this example. And yet, what I'm telling you on this particular strategy is that there are an unlimited number of things, each and every day that, don't have a lot of magnitude; things aren't that significant, at least in terms of how we normally think about significant gifts. Yet, the opportunity those gifts give us, to leverage our productivity and get things done, can be very significant.

Here's something interesting: with the person who gives you a $900 guitar, for example, there's almost an expectation on their part for a thank you note. I mean, that's almost $1,000 out of their pocket. So when they get a thank you note for something like that, it really doesn't have all that much impact because it was expected. However, when you send a thank you note for something, that, on the surface, doesn't appear to be that big of a deal, it makes a powerful and lasting impact.

Let me give you an example. A few years ago, I was in McDonald's in Trenton, Mo, standing in line behind a man and his wife. They were probably in their late 50's or early 60's, and they had stepped up to order something from the dollar menu like a couple of hamburgers, maybe some fries, and a couple of drinks. The cashier rang up the total and told him how much it would be, and I saw this guy in front of me patting the pockets on the back of his jeans; I saw this look of shock come across his face, as he's now feeling the pockets on his jacket, and he's feeling his shirt pockets.

He didn't have his wallet with him, and his wife was standing there without her purse. They had ordered, and then realized they had gone off and left their wallet and purse, or anything that might have had money in it, at home.

I happened to be standing right behind them and the total for their order was less than 6 dollars. I just stepped around the side of them, and I placed 6 dollars down near the cashier, saying, "Here, I've got it." Initially, the couple was like, "No, no, no...you don't need to do that." I said, "Look, you know what? If I can't buy somebody a meal who has left their wallet at home, then I don't know what I can do."

When I left McDonald's, in less than an hour I had forgotten what I had done for that couple. It really wasn't a big deal to me. I was there anyway and going to eat. I had money with me, so it wasn't that big of a deal. But to that couple, it was.

About a month later, I get this wonderful, hand-written note in the mail. It was a thank you card, but inside the thank you card was about a 2 page thank you letter. They had somehow tracked me down, finding out who I was and what my address was, and sent me a 2-page thank you note.

I ask you, how much is that worth? If you were a business owner or a parent of a child in a community, how much is that worth to you and your family? How much is that worth to the reputation of your family or reputation of your children?

It took less than 20 seconds and a total of 6 dollars for me to take care of that meal for them; a small act of kindness on my end. But, it was a big enough deal for them, again, because of the thing we talked about earlier. There's this correlation between the significance of the deed and likelihood somebody will send a thank you note. Because it was a simple $6 meal I helped them with, I had no expectation...none at all...of getting any kind of recognition for it later, and because I didn't expect it, it made the thank you note they sent, a BIG deal to me. A true win-win.

Where in your life, could you find a reason to send thank you notes? Could you send a thank you note to the person who delivers your mail each day? Just a note to let them know how much you appreciate that they always get your mailbox closed because sometimes it rains?

Could you send a thank you note to the waiter or waitress at your favorite coffee shop just to let them know how much you enjoy their cheerfulness each day? While we might think a waiter or waitress is really there just to make a paycheck, and earn a few tips, some people-including many waiters and waitresses-will do far more for recognition and acknowledgement than they will for a tip. Also, a tip is really a poor indicator of acknowledgement or how happy we were with them, because socially, we've been conditioned to think we "have" to or "should" leave a tip.

If you go into a restaurant and sit down, order and eat, unless it was just terrible, you leave a tip. So, to the waitress or waiter who is getting the tip, it's really not an indication of how you feel about them and their service.

Why not take the time to write out a hand-written note? In case you're wondering what this has to do with productivity, you'll find this theme cropping up over and over again. Anything that you or I have ever done, or will ever do, in one way or another, will involve other people. And to the degree that we have the cooperation of those people, we will get those things done.

Furthermore, the degree to which we get those things done, will be greater when we have the cooperation of others.

The easiest way that I've found to do that is to show your appreciation and gratitude to others. The most inexpensive, but most impressive way of doing that is simply send a hand-written thank you card. It's nice to always have a stack of thank you cards on hand. Any time somebody does something you appreciate, however simple it may be, send them a thank you card.

When people get a thank you note less than a couple of days after they've interacted with you, it really creates that "Wow!" experience for people.

What about gifts? How can you best incorporate gifts? When I wrote my first book, I sent out a couple hundred dollars worth of engraved Cross ink pens. There were some very key people in getting my book published; people who wrote endorsements for my book, The Productivity of the Epiphany. You may have heard that you can't judge a book by its cover, but as you may know, almost every book you've ever purchased, involved you judging the book, first, by the cover. That's just the way we do it. We look, and if the cover grabs our attention, only then will we pick it up and take a look inside.

Research shows that when somebody walks into a bookstore, if the spine or the face of the book grabs their attention, they will pick up the book. Then they will turn the book over and look at the back cover. If the back cover has captured their interest, then and only then, will they open the book up to see what's inside.

Once they have opened that book and there are endorsements from leaders in that particular field or in the area related to the topic of the book, that can set the tone for everything else that follows. I was fortunate to have some very key people write endorsements for my first book. Some very strong leaders in the area of personal development and productivity wrote endorsements for my book.

So, I went to the jewelry store, gave them a list of names of those who had written endorsements and had the names of each of these folks engraved on a nice Cross pen. I then mailed them each a copy of my book, when it was in print, along with the engraved pen.

Several of these people have written endorsements for a number of books, some of those books having been written by some big name, high level authors. I've had some of those people tell me that never in their life had they received a gift for writing an endorsement, other than maybe a copy of the book they had written it for. They had never received anything like a Cross pen with their name engraved on it. The fact that I had given them a personalized gift was something that really stood out in their mind, and will for years to come.

So be a note sender and a gift giver. Watch what happens with the cooperation you get from people as well as what happens to the number of people that are willing to cooperate with you. As a result, notice what happens to your productivity.

Strategy #13:

Review Your Day Each Evening

---

*"Sometimes, you have to look back in
order to understand the things that lie ahead"*
-YVONNE WOON

The way that I suggest you review your day each evening is wildly different from the way most people review their day. A lot of people not only review their day in the evening, but they review different parts of their day as the day goes on.

For example, maybe mid-morning, someone will review their day in terms of what went wrong. Then, they'll think about what went wrong again at noon, adding to that, what had gone wrong mid-morning. They do this over and over, so that throughout the entire day, they're constantly reviewing, beating themselves up for what went wrong or what was less than perfect, and by the time they get to bed at night and think back throughout their day, they have nothing but chaos and negative feelings to recall. Their entire focus is on every little thing that went wrong, and everything that didn't work out just as they had planned.

Research has long shown that visualization can play a big part in our future performance. When someone is replaying what went wrong and feeling bad about it all day, they're using the power of visualization to actually get better at repeating all of the things they didn't like; the things that went wrong.

The review at the end of the day that I'm going to be suggesting isn't about a "Pollyanna" "happy-go-lucky, everything is beautiful" type of thinking. You're still going to incorporate a review that initially involves the things that didn't work out as you wanted it to. However, from that point on, it gets radically different because as soon as you recall something that didn't work out the way you wanted, rather than just leaving that memory there to continue to play out in the future, you're going to rewind, so to speak; you're going to go back the beginning of that memory, and then you're going to replay it the way you would have liked it to work out.

Our brain and our unconscious responds to the cues that we provide. When we are continually and repeatedly remembering and replaying something that we viewed as a mistake, the unconscious says, "Hey, if that's what you want, that's what you're going to get." It's only going to give back, and only can give back, in terms of the data we give it to work with.

So let's just say, for example, something as simple as going to get coffee, and while doing that, you knocked the coffee pot over and spilled coffee all over a co-worker. That's a rather simple, and very common example. Most people would simply feel very embarrassed about that, and then when they thought back about their day, they would recall that, and see it in their mind the way it had played out. They would see that whole event repeat itself, and imagine spilling coffee all over the co-worker. They might do that again tomorrow; they might do that again next week. They might do that for several months. Each and every time they think about that particular day or that person, boom... it triggers the memory and they see it just like it happened. Not particularly useful.

Far more useful would be, the first time you recall that memory, you run that right back to the beginning. Run it back just before the beginning, and then simply ask the question, "If it had worked out well, what would that have looked like?" and simply imagine that.

Sometimes when you tell somebody that you want them to visualize something, they get all hung up on this thing of, "I can't. I've tried to visualize before and I just can't." Sometimes, it's the very word, "visualize" that tenses people up. If I asked you to think about the car that you would like to have some day, you wouldn't look at me and say, "Well, I can't. I've tried to think about that before and I'm just not able to." You would simply go inside your head and probably in just a few seconds, you'd say, "Oh, it's a Ferrari," or "It's a Cadillac," or "It's a Corvette." Whatever it was, you wouldn't say, "Oh, I don't have the ability to think about it."

Visualizing can also be thought of as simply "thinking" about something. In the evening, right before bed, you're just going to think about your day: you're going to think about the things that didn't work out as you had wanted them to, and then you're going to think about or imagine what it would have looked like if it were perfect.

What have we done at this point? You will have told your brain, in so many words, "Not this, THIS!" However, when you do the old way, instead, and you go back and replay the mistake, what you're saying to your brain is, "This is what I want you to focus on. This is what I want you to repeat for me. This is what I want you to make easier to happen the next time." That is not a good idea.

It really doesn't take long for your brain to understand what it is you want. You don't want to repeat the mistake. Instead you want the alternative that you're providing with your imagination. So after you've looked at the mistake-what you don't want to repeat-you're going to focus on what you do want, so only look at the mistake once. Then, rewind to just prior to when the mistake started, and provide the alternative.

What would it have looked like if it turned out the way you wanted? When you are clear on the answer to that, then you want to play that in your head multiple times; showing your unconscious what you *do* want to be doing next time.

What are some areas in your life where you could use this? What about in your relationships? Is there a conversation? Is there some type of interaction or communication that you've been engaged in with someone that worked out less than favorable? Rather than beat yourself up by replaying it over and over again and feeling bad about it, replay it once, then rewind it to the very beginning, and put in the alternative. How would it have looked if it worked out just the way you wanted it to? What would you have said? How would you have been using your body? What would their facial expressions look like? What would their posture look like? What about their comments to you? What would the outcome be if it worked out exactly like you had wanted it to? When you know, replay that several times.

Remember, you're telling your brain, "Not this, THIS!" Once

your brain gets what the "THIS" is, it makes it so much easier for you to find yourself just naturally engaging in that response, in the future. The best time to do this is right before you go to bed.

The last thought, or series of thoughts you have just before you fall asleep every night are likely the thoughts that are really going to be most relevant. That's what your brain is going to work with, right after you fall asleep.

Do your daily review. You'll probably be able to do this in the last 5 minutes before you close your eyes and go to sleep. You're going to do your review and editing. You'll eventually get to the point where this streamlines so much that you'll be able to do this entire thing in less than 60 seconds, because your brain has that kind of capability. It's the same brain that's experienced an entire day in a matter of seconds, in a dream.

Strategy #14:

Do at Least One Thing Each Day Out of Your Comfort Zone

"The further you get away from yourself, the more challenging it is. Not to be in your comfort zone is great fun"
-BENEDICT CUMBERBATCH

That doesn't sound like a very comfortable thing to do; to do something out of your comfort zone, does it? John Grinder, one of the co-developers of Neuro Linguistic Programming, or NLP, said, "The key to success is learning to be comfortable being uncomfortable." Initially, that sounded very strange to me. I thought, "Be comfortable about being uncomfortable? What are you talking about? How do you do that?"

John went on to explain that most people feel very uncomfortable about feeling uncomfortable. So when they start to feel uncomfortable, they feel uncomfortable about that and they move away from whatever it is. If you think about anything that you're able to do today, or anything that you know today, in terms of knowledge or a particular skill set, when you first started it was really uncomfortable. In fact, John Grinder proposes, if we "learn" something and it's not a little bit uncomfortable, or we don't experience some degree of confusion, that we really haven't learned anything new. All new learning is preceded by confusion, which is uncomfortable.

If it was comfortable, it would mean we haven't learned something new, we've just been exposed to something we already knew, but has been repackaged a little differently, which is why it's so comfortable, because we already knew and had the foundation for it in our head. All real new learning is preceded by confusion and a degree of discomfort.

If you will look at anything in your life that you have set out to do; any goal, whether it be a project you are working on personally for your own company or for your own business, or perhaps a company that you are employed with now, or have been in the past, the sticking point, or the plateau, almost invariably comes down to those moments where you start to feel uncomfortable. That's where you start to pull back, and where all forward movement stops. You start to ease back and drift back to what's familiar, and then, everything feels better.

How do you develop this skill; this ability to learn to feel comfortable about being uncomfortable? As strange as it may sound, initially, the key is found in the word, "about." With that one word, "about", we can learn to instantly shift up a level and have any feeling, emotion, or state about previous feeling, emotion, or state.

Here's an example. If you tell me, "You know, Vince, I'm feeling kind of depressed," and I say, "Well, how do you feel about that?" you might say, "Well, I feel kind of bad about that." This is an example of you feeling bad about feeling depressed. But watch what happens. I ask "You feel kind of bad about feeling depressed, and how do you feel about that?"

You answer, "That's probably not a very useful thing for me to do." We're already making progress. We moved from thoughts and feelings about being depressed to feeling bad about feeling depressed, and with two questions, we've already arrived at a place where you're saying, "Feeling bad about feeling depressed is probably not really a useful thing."

So I say, "You probably feel that feeling bad about feeling depressed is probably not a useful place to be." And you say, "Yeah, that's right. " Then I say, "What do you feel about that thought, or that understanding?" You say, "I feel pretty good about that because just being able to realize that feeling bad about it is not useful, it puts me in a place of having a choice of being able to decide to do something different."

The best part? I didn't provide you with any knowledge, suggestions, or tools. I simply asked you "How do you feel about that?" Whatever the answer was, I said, "How do you feel about that?" And so on, and so forth, until eventually, you started to pop into a more positive and more useful way of thinking about those initial thoughts and feelings of being depressed.

Let's apply this to feeling uncomfortable about something, in particular. Let's say that you've decided to go back to school. Maybe you graduated in 1978, and it's been a long time, but hey, you're going to go back to school and are going to get that degree. It's coming up on that first day of school and you're really starting to feel anxious and nervous, and you're having a cup of coffee, and I say, "Really, you're really anxious and nervous?" You say, "Oh my Gosh, yes!" I say, "How do you feel about it?" You say, "Well, I don't know. It's really new. I guess maybe it's to be expected, feeling anxious and nervous about going back to school after you haven't been there for 30 years."

I say, "Yeah, yeah. I agree with you. They're probably pretty normal thoughts and how do you feel about that? How do you feel about having normal thoughts about going back to school?" You answer, "Well, I guess it just means that I'm human and I'm probably doing the right thing. It's always something I've wanted to do." Whatever it is you are going to say, by using a question, "How do you feel about that feeling, or about that thought?" it's allowed you to start thinking in a different perspective.

Einstein always said that a problem can never be solved on the same level on which it exists. I never understood that, and of course that wasn't too surprising. I mean, you've got one of the most brilliant men in the world making the statement. I guess it would stand to reason that mere mortals like me would have a little bit of tough time understanding that. However, I eventually did come to understand what he was talking about.

Einstein said, "A problem cannot be solved on the level of which it exists, or where the thinking about it exists." If you're thinking about your thoughts and feelings of being uncomfortable, Einstein was right. You can't solve the feelings of being uncomfortable at the level of uncomfortable thoughts. You have to rise to a different level; you have to get higher and get above those thoughts. How do you do that?

It's simple. You can ask yourself that question. "I'm uncomfortable about going back to school. I'm a nervous, anxious wreck. I don't know if I should do this or not." Step away and ask yourself, "How do I feel about those kinds of feelings? How do I feel about that kind of thinking?"

If you're experiencing anxiety, say, "How do I feel about that?" Very quickly, your mind will come up with an answer like, "Well, it's probably not a very useful feeling to have right now and there's probably a better state or emotion or feeling to be experiencing." Ask the question again about the answer to that, "Well how do I feel about that?" "I feel pretty good about that because coming to the realization that there's something better means that I realize that there's something more enjoyable for me."

The key word is "about". "How do I feel ABOUT that thought, that feeling, that behavior?"

Here's something I started doing years ago. If you'll think about it, a cashier at a grocery store is in a very routine and often monotonous situation. Not everybody that comes through their line is in a grand mood. Sometimes people are downright cranky. It's often not the most pleasant experience in the world for these people who are standing there, taking money and scanning groceries all day. And believe me when I tell you that they are receptive and open to anybody who can come along, put a smile on their face, make them feel good about themselves, and just lighten their load, even if just for a few minutes.

Almost every cashier in every grocery store in the United States is wearing a nametag. I long ago realized that almost everybody who wears a nametag, every day, very quickly forgets that they're wearing one. It's something that's there, but they don't feel it anymore. They don't look down at it; it's only other people looking at it. So, the person wearing it forgets that it's there.

So, when I would come through the grocery line, out of my peripheral vision, I would glance at their nametag. Maybe their nametag says "Lisa." And so, the initial greeting with a cashier is, "Hello, how are you today? Did you find everything all right?" Of course, I'd say, "Yes." And with a very serious look on my face, I would say, "Is there a Lisa that works here? Is there a cashier by the name of Lisa?" And, immediately, they would get this very serious look on their face, like, "Oh my gosh, what's going on? What's wrong? What happened?" And they'd say, "Yes, I'm Lisa." And at that point, I would just point to their nametag and say, "Yes, I guess you are. It says so right there." They would kind of have this moment of laughter...and a realization that they had forgotten that they had a nametag on their shirt.

You see, up until that point, their mind was screaming, "How in the world would this guy know my name is Lisa? There must be something wrong or they wouldn't be looking for a Lisa" Why would I do this?

See, we get so stuck in this rut of thinking that everything we say or do has to either be logical or something that a "normal" person would do. That's the type of rigidity that keeps people from exploring their dreams, from pursuing their passions, from being as productive as they can be.

The whole point of telling you the story that had no point was to see that by doing things that aren't necessarily logical, that invite others into this little dance of breaking up the monotony of their day, it's something that is appreciated by them, and it's conditioning your mind...it's conditioning your nervous system, to start doing things just for the sake of doing them, and not just because they make sense; not just because that's what everybody else does.

If you do what everybody else does, you're going to experience and have what everybody else has. If what everybody else is doing and experiencing is what you want, then that can be good. But in most cases, what other people are doing and experiencing is not what you want to have to do, or feel.

So, let your mind run wild with the unlimited number of ways and things that you can do each day that lie outside your comfort zone. Will it be easy to do? No! If it is, then it's inside your comfort zone and it defeats the whole purpose of the exercise.

Pick things that are fun or would be fun, that you're uncomfortable doing. Do them anyway. If you find that you're getting hung up and say, "You know, I'm supposed to but I can't because I'm too uncomfortable." Then run yourself through the "How do I feel about that?" question. Go through that in as many steps as you have to until you get to a place where all of a sudden, you feel the tension just go, POOF!

Let me tell you, that is a key, a critical piece, in becoming more productive because to really reach the pinnacle of being a productive human being, it's going to involve doing things that you're not currently doing or that you've never done before. Therefore, they would have a tendency to be uncomfortable. If you are uncomfortable about being uncomfortable, that means you'll always do what you've done. That's not what you want and that's not the way to move forward towards increased productivity.

Strategy #15:

Adopt the "If I'm on Time, I'm Late" Philosophy

"I figured this was the easy stuff, and if we couldn't show up on time, looking right and acting right, we weren't going to be able to do anything else"
-BO SCHEMBECHLER

I can think of nothing that does as much to bolster your reputation with others in your field, with your friends, family, colleagues, and other people you do business with, as never being late; being known as someone who is always punctual.

First, we should examine why so many people are not on time. I think the heart of it often comes down to thinking of being on time as "being on time." For example, if they're supposed to be some place at 8:00am, then they think that if they're there at 8:00am, they're on time. The problem with that is this: if they live, let's say, 30 minutes away from their destination, their reasoning is, if I leave at 7:30am, if I'm supposed to be there at 8:00am, and I leave my home, which is 30 minutes away, at 7:30am, then I will be on time.

The challenge is that they are frequently going to experience a situation where they're going to leave their home at 7:30 in the morning so they can be at their 8:00 appointment, which is just 30 minutes from their home...but.. on this morning there's the driver in front of them with a flat tire, or they have a flat tire; there's the wreck that reroutes traffic, there's always something that adds five or ten minutes to that 30 minute drive that they had planned on.

And what happens? Rather than being there at 8:00am, which was when the appointment was, you're there at 8:05am, or you're there at 8:10am. Both of those are late. Both of those are times in which other people who are waiting on you are going to look at and say, "Oh, they're late." You know, isn't it interesting when somebody is late, it's not like there are varying degrees of lateness?

There is if you're the person who is late and you try to minimize it by saying, "Yeah, I'm just a little bit late." Put yourself on the other side; if you're the person waiting on someone, you know there's no such thing as a degree of lateness. They're either on time or they're late. They are the only one that will be saying things like, "I was a little bit late", or "Sorry, running a little late." There's either on time, or there's late.

If you're the person waiting, and they're on time, it's comforting. If they're late, even if it's one minute late, it's very distracting.

So what do you do, then? One strategy that many people use, although not as successfully as you might think, people try to factor in a little bit of time for some of the things that could go wrong.

The problem with that is this you have no way of knowing what could go wrong. We don't know if there's going to be an accident that's going to result in us being rerouted and having a 5 minute delay, or if there's going to be an accident that's going to involve us being rerouted or waiting in traffic, that is going to result in a 30 minute delay. When we try to plan for the delays, we're making a critical error, because we can't know what those delays will be.

Planning for delays is not a good model to pursue. What do we do then? The model that I have used for over 25 years now has kept me from ever being late. Does that mean I'm more intelligent? Does that mean I'm smarter? No. What it means is I'm using a model that a great many people do not use, and it works.

Here's the model. If I'm on time, I'm late. It's as simple as that. If I'm supposed to be some place at 8:00am and I show up at 8:00am, in my mind, I am late. Now, I might be on time in somebody else's eyes who is waiting on me to show up at 8:00am, but in my mind, I'm late. What does that do? If in my mind, I'm going to be late if I get there at 8:00am, then I have to decide what is going to count as being on time for me. I'll give you some of the parameters that I use, and you'll have to come up with your own time parameters.

I would urge you to be very liberal with them. I would urge you to create very wide time parameters. Again, because you can't guess, you can't judge or determine or predict ahead of time, what delays you might encounter. This is different than trying to factor in delays. In fact, it's not even thinking about delays. It's simply stating to yourself "if I'm on time, I'm late, therefore, for me, to consider myself on time what will be the parameter that

I use?"

I have a 100-mile drive from my house to the airport that I typically fly from in Kansas City, MO. From the moment I leave my driveway until I pull into the parking lot at the Kansas City airport, it's exactly 100 miles. It will typically take me an hour and forty-five minutes to drive that 100 miles. Now, a lot of times, different airlines will suggest different times, to make sure you're there before your flight time, but let's just go with one hour. Certain airlines suggest that you should be there an hour before your flight. That would be on time for most people. That would be on time for the airlines. But my criteria is at least 2 hours before my flight.

If I were to arrive at the airport 1 hour before my flight was going to take off, in my mind, I'm an hour late, which means I adjust the time that I'm going to leave my home by a minimum of at least an hour, so I get there at least 2 hours before. Now, what does that do?

First of all, it removes a tremendous amount of stress in my life. People who are running on time, or on what they call "on time" have no room for error; none whatsoever. If someone has 100 miles to drive, and they leave their driveway so that they'll be there the suggested 1 hour before their flight, and something happens that they didn't plan for, they are now thrown off by 10, 15, or 20 minutes. If during that 10, 15 or 20 minute period, their attention, their anxiety, and their frustration level is building, making it almost impossible for them to think clearly about what they need to do, then it is even more likely that they're going to be late.

I don't experience that for one reason: I have a belief that says

"If I'm on time, I'm late." So, I readjust what "on time" means to me. At a bare minimum, to arrive on time, you have to leave on time; if you have to be some place at 8:00am, and you're 30 minutes away by car, you should leave by at least 7:30am. To arrive on time, you have to leave on time.

People who are chronically late use this model: They say, "I should leave now, but what I'm going to do is leave in 10 minutes, and then hurry."

Do you know anybody like that? Do you know anybody who knows when they should leave, but they continually tell themselves, "I know I should leave now, but I'm going to leave in 10 minutes or in 15 minutes, and then I'll hurry." If this person is somebody close to you, or this happens to be you, you've likely discovered that you can't leave late and make up that time. It almost never works out. You can almost never compress the amount of time that you waited beyond when you should have left, so that you can arrive on time.

And in those rare situations where you are able to compress that time, you will arrive in a very unsafe manner, bringing potential risk to the other people around you on the roadway.

Play with the time parameters. Clearly, they'll be earlier than what they had been in the past. You should begin in small increments like 10 or 15 minutes earlier, and work your way up to 30 minutes, or even an hour. I can promise you one thing, you'll experience less stress in your day. Your reputation in terms of being somebody that's punctual and on time will be radically different a year from now than it is right now. You'll have more people extending more trust to you, because they'll know, if you say you're going to be there at a certain time, you will be there.

No questions asked.

Strategy #16:

Box Yourself in For Success

"A body of men holding themselves accountable to nobody ought not to be trusted by anybody"
-THOMAS PAINE

You're going to like this one because it matches up so well with something we talked about earlier when we were talking about establishing new habits. We talked about the fact that 21 days, as it turns out, just was not enough time to really groove it deeply at a neurological level. While it was a good start, 21 days was not enough as you know from possibly having done that in the past. If you slack off after 21 days, that previous habit was right there waiting. It was still easier to do and engage in than the new habit you had been trying to establish.

We talked about the fact that 90 days was really what it would take to create the grooves in your nervous system so that it was just as accessible to you, and just as likely that you would engage in the new habit as the previous habit.

"Box yourself in" has to do with creating a chart: creating a row of boxes. You can create a row of 10 boxes, or 3 rows of 10 boxes etc. The number of boxes you create really doesn't matter because after you've used the 10 boxes, you can create 10 more. I prefer to use 30 boxes at a time. And it comes down to this; each day you've completed the new action or whatever it is you wish to establish as a new habit, you take a pen, and color in the box for that particular day.

Let's say that a day comes up that you get "too busy" or you get sidetracked. Whatever it is, at the end of the day, you realize that this new habit you've been working on, didn't get done that day. If that's the case, you leave that square blank and don't color it in. You'll quickly learn that your mind does not like to see bare or naked blocks, and that you don't like how it feels.

You'll also learn that what your brain loves to see is a string of consecutive colored boxes. Once you've colored in 2 days in a row, you'll want a third. Let's say that third day in a row doesn't happen. You don't complete that task and so you have to leave it bare. Now you're working from both sides. You're working from the part of you that loves to color them in and likes how that looks, and you're also bringing in the part of you that does not like to see those empty squares.

What will happen is you'll eventually create a chain. You'll have 6 consecutive days, maybe you'll have 10 consecutive days, maybe even 20 consecutive days. and then, out of the blue, you miss a day and have to leave on blank. You won't like it, and that's great. The idea here is to have this in front of you where you have to look at it, because if we don't have this row of blocks that we color in or leave empty, depending on whether we complete the action or the behavior...if we don't have that, and we're just keeping track of this in our mind, you know as well as I do that it's very easy to push out of your mind, the memory of the days you didn't do it, and focus only on those that you have.

At the end of the month, maybe you've only engaged in the task or behavior 4 times, maybe 5 times, there will be well over 20 times that month that you didn't engage in the task. When somebody asks you how you're doing on this new project, new goal, or new habit, something predictable happens.

Immediately, your mind grabs on to the days that you did engage in this task, project, or new habit, and you say, "Oh, you know, pretty well. I think I'm doing pretty well." If you have on your wall next to your desk, or in your bedroom, or in the bathroom next to the mirror, this chart of blocks some place where you will have to look at it every day, that shows a string of empty non-colored boxes, it's hard to push that out of your mind because it's right there and it's staring back at you.

Get this out of your head and put it on paper and put it on a wall or somewhere else you can see it; where you have irrefutable evidence of days you've engaged in this task, and how many day you have not.

At some point, you'll go over what I call "the hump." Once you've gotten over the hump, you'll have a certain number of days back to back and you will not, at all cost, want to break that chain. It's just as simple as that. After you've had 5 or 6 of those days, you maybe don't want to break that chain, but it's not at the over "the hump" point yet, because something comes up and you'll allow yourself to get off track for a day. You don't like it, and not liking it, is good for you.

I don't know what the magic number will be for you. It could be 12, it could be 15, it could be 20, but the day will come when you know you're over the hump because you will be compelled, you will be driven, you will see the blocks colored in, all back to back, and you'll have this overwhelming drive and feeling to not break the chain.

When you feel that in the pit of your stomach, you know you're over the hump. You'll also know that once you get to the 90 day mark, and you've got row after row after row of colored in blocks, not only at a conscious level do you know you're over the hump, but also you'll know you're over the hump on an unconscious and a neurological level, and that's a good place to be.

Strategy #17:

Your Mind Will Process Faster Than You Think

"The world as we have created it is a process of our thinking. It cannot be changed without changing our thinking"

-ALBERT EINSTEIN

Have you ever hit a plateau? Where things seem like they come to a grinding halt, and suddenly, you feel stuck? As you know, from previous experience, if you feel stuck for too long, you start to get frustrated; and when you get frustrated, your creativity starts to short circuit, and your productivity falls off sharply.

Usually when we plateau and feel stuck, it has a lot less to do with what's going on in our external environment, and has more to do with some type of challenge we have internally.

It could be a limiting belief you have about your abilities or what you believe you can accomplish, or about somebody else's capabilities or abilities. It could be any number of things going on in your head.

I'm sure you've had the experience of trying to think your

way through these challenges in the past. While that sounds like a good idea, at first, it really comes down to *how* you are trying to think your way through the inner chaos.

Most of the time, we think very slowly, lingering excessively on things we can do very little about. While there are times in life where that's useful, it very actively engages the logical part of our brain- the pre-frontal cortex. This is the part of our brain that scrutinizes every single thought, and is quick to say, "No, that won't work" about a potentially creative thought that pops up.

An idea that could be useful comes to mind, and all of a sudden, the analytical part of the brain says. "No!! That won't work!" Many times, those thoughts that come to mind would work if we just got them out on paper; if we just let the thought germinate and allowed it to blossom into the grander idea that's within the seed of the initial thought. It's that logical, analytical, critical thinking of the pre-frontal cortex that comes in and squashes everything down.

So what do you do? Remember your mind will process faster than you think, so you have to engage your mind in a way that allows it to process as fast as it's able to. The only reason we don't do that is because we try to sit down and think things through slowly, which takes us in the opposite direction we want to go in if we want to recruit the full power of our mind. To get the most out of our brain, we've got to let it run as fast as it can.

How do you do that? The simplest way I've found to do that is to first write down your challenge, or the area that is causing the most frustrations, at the top of a piece of paper.

You don't write down the problem, "My problem is..." You

write down your problem or your challenge *in the form of a question*. Why? Once we have made a statement about something, our brain just shuts off.

The unconscious mind processes statements as conclusions. If a conclusion has been drawn about something, why continue processing? However, the unconscious mind processes questions much differently. When we ask a question, our brain starts searching through all of our past experiences, memories and stored information for an answer, as well as our external environment, for any pieces of the puzzle that might be found, there. We literally prime our brain in a way that helps it create answers, anytime we remember to ask questions.

Robert Kiyosaki, in the book, Rich Dad, Poor Dad, said that his rich father forbade them from ever making the statement, "I can't afford it." You were likely told, or heard someone in your household say, "We can't afford it!"...I heard that often when I was growing up, as well. So, we grow up with that, and it seems like such a logical thing, that we begin thinking and saying "I can't afford it" when we see something we want, and look in our wallet and see that we have less than the item costs. By default, we blurt out, "Man...I want that, but I can't afford it!" We know what happens when we make that statement, and the conclusion that is perceived by our unconscious mind.

Kiyosaki said his rich father demanded that when they discovered they didn't have enough money for something they really wanted, that they ask the question, "How can I afford it?"

This kind of question is the difference that makes the difference. Remember, the thought or statement "I can't afford it," which shuts the mind off; as far as your unconscious mind is concerned, it's done and over with. However, the *question*, "*How can* I afford it?*" kicks the unconscious mind into overdrive, and it starts churning immediately so that it can produce a series of answers to the question. Kiyosaki's rich father knew that when you present the unconscious with a *question*, it will process, look, scan, and search, for the answer to your question, and given enough time, it will find one... maybe several.

After you've written down what you desire at the top of the paper, in the form of question, such as "how can I generate $1000 in the next 6 days?" or " How can I create a stronger relationship with my wife ?" just look at it for a moment, perhaps reading it out loud a couple of times, and then just go about your business. Forget about whether you know the answer to the question, or not . If it's really a problem or challenge, one that's really had you stymied, then the chances are you will have no idea at that time.

Don't write this question down thinking that as soon as you do, there will immediately be an answer. That will not be the case, most of the time. The best thing you can do is just step away, mentally, emotionally, and physically. I like to pose the question and then walk away from it completely for at least 24 hours.

After that 24-hour period, I get a pen, eliminate all distractions -like the television or the radio- sit down at the table, and get out this paper that has the question I had written down. We can use the example, "How can I generate $1000 in the next 6 days?" You're going read the question you had written down and walked away from for at least 24 hours, and then you're going to immediately start writing 50 answers as quickly as possible; you're not going to stop and think about them; you're not going to write one and say, "Does that make sense?" You're just going to write, write, write, write, write as fast as you can.

Are you going to have some crazy things pop out on that paper? Absolutely; but you're also going to have some brilliant ideas come out, that when you're finished and you look back, you're going to say, "Holy cow! I would have never thought of that!" You'll get solid ideas that would never have come to mind if you were trying to think "logically."

I am a huge advocate of logical and critical thinking, and believe that most people don't do enough of it in key areas. However, when it comes to creativity and getting beyond a problem or challenge, often times what we find the logical, analytical, and critical part of our mind gets in the way. It blocks and shuts down our creativity.

Why does this work like it does? It's real simple. You're going faster than your critical and analytical mind can keep up. Going fast literally overloads the conscious mind. As a result, you tap into the vast network of information created, and gathered by, your unconscious mind.

Strategy #18:

Get Rid of All But Three of Your Email Folders

---

*"You will never reach your destination if you stop and throw
stones at every dog that barks"*
—WINSTON CHURCHILL

For some of you, that probably causes instant panic to think
about that; to get rid of all but 3 of your email folders. I'm going
to explain why, but first let's talk about the average number of
folders that someone might have if they're using folders. It's not
uncommon at all, when I'm doing my workshops and seminars
to have people start stressing when I tell them to do this.

What I find is that there are some things that are consistent,
no matter where you go, in human behavior. In my seminars I
ask, "Of those of you using folders, how many of you have more
than 10 folders?" Several hands go up. Then I ask, "More than
20?" Several hands go up. There are many people I have found
that have 30 or 40 folders that they use to take the emails that
make it to their inbox.

We talked about earlier, how the human mind, in terms of

consciousness, cannot hold more than 5 to 9 chunks of information at any given time. If it goes beyond that, then the communication or information causes the brain to go into overwhelm and that's when anxiety, feelings of panic, and fear kick in.

I've had people almost flip when I first shared this strategy of just using 3 folders. Before they even know why or how it's utilized, they're already shaking their head "no." Internally, they're thinking "That's not possible, and that's just going to cause me more confusion and disorganization than anything I can think of." Nothing can be further from the truth. Typically, when people have 10, 15, 20, or 40 folders, they don't know how to effectively use the search function in the email program that they're using.

The moment you know the search function will work for you, you're ready to let go of having multiple folders; you know that having 3 can do what you were doing before with multiple folders, and do it with much less stress.

The search function on your email program allows you to perform a search on your email program that will pull up for you, all of the emails that have the search word/s that you're searching for.

For example, if you are looking for an email that came from Mrs. Roberta King, and you're not sure what folder it's in, it's not a problem, you just type Mrs. Roberta King or even Roberta, or Roberta King, or just King, into that search function, and it will bring up every email that has those search words.

This is what makes it possible to just have 3 folders. You can label your 3 folders anything you choose. In fact, it would probably be better if you personalize the way you label them or what you call them. It's what they're designed to *do* that matters.

My folders are named:

1. Treasure Chest

2. Action Required

3. Not Sure Yet

Any time an email comes to my email inbox, the moment I open it, it's either going to go to one of those 3 folders, or it will be deleted. The way I determine what I'm going to do with it is by knowing the function of the 3 folders.

For example, the Treasure Chest folder is for emails that I may want to keep indefinitely. I may need to reference them a year from now. I might need to reference them 5 years from now. I just know that I want them long-term.

If it's an email that's going to require something like a phone call a week from now, or require me to send out a letter, or require any type of follow-up at all, that I'm not going to do at that moment, it's going to the Action Required folder.

I refuse, at this point in my life, to open up an email, look at it, and then leave it lingering in my inbox. If every time you open up your email and you've got 5000 emails sitting in your inbox, that is overwhelming to your nervous system and overwhelming to your unconscious mind. It causes unnecessary stressing.

Every time I leave and exit my email, when I come back and open it up, anything that is going to be in my inbox is going to be something I have not seen before. It won't be something that I looked at yesterday or last week or last month or, in some cases, six months ago. It will not be there. This eliminates a lot of confusion.

The third folder that I use is simply called, Not Sure Yet. Not Sure Yet includes emails that may have a follow-up action, but there is just not enough information right now for me to determine for sure whether or not it's going to require a follow-up action. It might be something that I'm going to want to put in my Treasure Chest. There is just not enough information in this email at this particular time for me to decide.

Any email that comes to my email inbox is either going to be deleted, go to the Treasure Chest folder, my Action Required folder, or it's going to the Not Sure Yet folder. That's it. It's only going to one of those 3 folders or it's going to be deleted.

If you've been used to using more than 3 folders, thinking that it was a lot easier for you, because all you had to do was find the right folder and then open it up, then at first, this is going to feel very odd. But after you get past the very brief and initial newness of this system, you'll be thrilled with the ease it creates in instantly knowing what to do with each email in your inbox.

There is a fourth folder that we're going to talk about that you will need *temporarily*. I'm guessing that you're going to need this folder, initially, because if you're like many of the people I talk to, you have lots of emails sitting in your inbox right now.

If you try to go through hundreds of emails in your email inbox, opening them up again for the second time, looking at them one at a time, sorting them, deciding "Do they get deleted, or do they go into my Treasure Chest? Do they go into my Action Required or do they go into Not Sure Yet?", that's going to take quite a while to do. In the meantime, you've got new emails that are coming in. It can be overwhelming. It's like heavy snow, piling up faster than you can shovel it. Therefore, it is critical that you take everything that's in your email inbox now, and create a folder that's called Instant Relief.

Create this Instant Relief folder and you take every email that's currently in your inbox, whether it be 10 or whether it be 10,000, and you put them all in this *temporary* folder.

When you have completed that, you now, perhaps for the first time in your life, have an empty inbox.

From this point on, every email that comes in, if you open it, you commit to also deciding what to do with it. In fact, never open another email again in your life unless you are willing to commit to deciding, at that moment, what to do with that email. Whatever your decision may be, you know it's not going to include leaving it in the inbox. If you open any email, it's going to be deleted, it's going to the Treasure Chest long term, it's going to the Action Required, or it's going to Not Sure Yet.

The only way you can get to this stage or you can start implementing this with ease is to clear out your inbox right now. You say, "Well wait a minute, Vince, there might be some really important emails in my inbox right now. Some that I need to get to, and if I cram them all in this Instant Relief, and just start working from the new emails that are coming in, I might not get to them. I might not see them."

Here's the solution. Set aside a time each day, whether it be five, ten, or thirty minutes; decide on a length of time each day where you will do one thing and one thing only-open up the Instant Relief folder, and go through and open the emails that are in that file. Then you will decide to either delete, move them to Treasure Chest, move them to Action Required, or they will go to the Not Sure Yet category.

This may seem like, "Oh, Vince, if I have over 1000 put into my Instant Relief folder, I'll never get through them." The only reason it seemed like before you would never get through them all is because you had them in the inbox where there were constantly new emails adding to them, so it seemed like you were never able to get ahead.

That's not the case, now, because you will never again have any more in your Instant Relief folder than you do when you moved them there. If you delete 5, or if you move 5 of them, then you have 5 fewer in that folder, and you will go through in that fashion until the Instant Relief folder is empty. You have made a decision about every email that was in that folder. You either deleted it, moved it to Treasure Chest, Action Required, or Not Sure Yet. When you've gone through them all, it's empty, and then you get rid of that folder.

Now you have only 3 folders: Treasure Chest, Action Required, Not Sure Yet. I can tell you that if you make the decision today, this is going to be one of the habits that you happily build into your neurology so that it's automatic. You will never be able to fathom how you got along without this system before.

Strategy #19:

Learn to Say "No"

"Tone is the hardest part of saying no"
-JONATHAN PRICE

Many people have a hard time saying, "No", and it causes them a lot of problems—problems that could be avoided.

I can't tell you how many times I've had people come up to me, either on a break, or at lunch during a seminar, and pull me aside, wanting to talk to me about their inability, or what they think of as an inability, to say "no." Sometimes they're people, who, on the outside, appear to be very authoritative and firm people. In some situations, they probably are, and yet, they find themselves in one situation after another, where it would be useful to them- in terms of their productivity- to be able to say "no."

Instead, they're in this loop of not being able to say no, and it's cutting into their productivity, business and personal life, and they don't know how to get out of it by themselves.

One of the first things I point out, is that they *are* saying "no", they just don't realize it, yet. See, anything we say "yes" to, we are also, at the same time, saying "no" to an unlimited number of *other* things we could be doing during that same period of time.

Whatever somebody is paying you to do each hour of the day, they are also paying you to *not* be doing other things. That's why it is so relevant, so crucial, and so important to be passionate about what you do, and love the way you earn your income. You should want to wake up each morning and want to get out of bed, and to be staying up later than you should each night, having to force yourself to go to bed because you can't keep yourself from working on something that applies to what you're passionate about and what you love.

If you are looking at the clock at the end of the day saying "I get to go home in an hour," or "I get to go home in five minutes," that should be your first indication that you're not passionate about your job and aren't overly excited about what you do.

Sometimes somebody will tell me, "Hey, I just got this new job. I'm going to be making $30 an hour." Notice, they skip right over telling me what the job is-what they will be doing for that $30 an hour- it's almost as if it doesn't matter.

They get excited about how much they're going to be paid an hour. Remember, anytime we are being paid to do something, we are also being paid to *not* be doing anything else during that same time. They're being paid $30 an hour to *not* be doing other things during each of those hours. If they're at that job 10 hours a day, getting paid $30 an hour, that's $300 a day. They have agreed to take $300 a day in exchange for *not* doing anything else during those 10 hours except this one thing. If you love what you're doing during those 10 hours, that's great. If not, have you considered what you're being paid *not* to do? Most people focus on only what they're being paid to do.

When you begin to focus on, and think about what you're being paid *not* to do, sometimes, just like that, you say, "Oh my gosh, there's my passion! There's my love. There's my family. There's my kids. There's this, there's that, and I'm being paid *not* to do all of those things because all of those things take place during the time I'm paid to do my job and to *not* do the things I love!"

Learn to say "no", and in case you can't tell, yes, I am absolutely passionate about learning to say "no", about teaching people to say "no", because fewer things get in the way of enjoying life, than not being able to say "no" to the things you don't really want to be doing.

There are 3 typical answers that you can give when someone asks you to do something. Let's say the phone rings and your good friend Alice asks, "Hey, would you like to join this new committee? I'd really like for you to be on this committee with me. I think you'd make some really nice contributions to the group. It's a very important cause." They start to layer on the guilt about how important the cause is, and when they ask you to join this committee, there are basically three answers you can give.

1. "No"

2. "Yes"

3. "Maybe"

Let's look at these, starting with "maybe." The moment you have told someone "maybe" about anything, whatever it is you have been asked to do, it's going to occupy a massive amount of mental and emotional space in your mind. It's going to keep circulating and whipping through your mind, taking up this mental RAM, if you will, because you've not given it a home. You've not made a decision, so until such time, it's going to occupy a great deal of your consciousness and unconscious space, and it's just there. It's mental clutter.

Now let's look at "yes." Somebody says, "Do you want to join this? Do you want to do this? Will you do this?" The moment you say "yes", you kick your creativity into gear because it serves as a launching pad for you to begin.

"Maybe" doesn't do that. "Yes", however, serves as this thick, sturdy foundation from which you can begin creating, thinking, and you can begin deciding about actions."Maybe" is an "if." "If" I do this. "If" I decide to go there. The moment you say "yes" it moves it from "if" to "how." You begin asking "how?" I don't ask "how" questions about things that I've said "maybe" to. I only ask "how", and therefore begin to generate the answers I need, after I have said "yes." So if you want to be able to move from "if" to "how", you've got to move from "maybe" to "yes."

However, we're focusing on the "no" aren't we? What does "no" do? "No" clears the space for something else, and that's it. "Maybe" occupies space, "yes" takes up space, but it launches you into creativity, so it can be useful space. "Maybe" just takes up gray space and nothing happens. A nice, firm "no" clears space, or keeps that space clear; not only in your head, but on your schedule.

Let me say that again. A "no" keeps space clear in your head and therefore on your schedule.

Michael Neil, author of several books, and a brilliant coach, says to take a piece of paper and pen and draw three lines so that you've got three equal sections. You've got a left hand column, a middle column and a right hand column. At the top of the left far column, write "yes." Then go over to the far right, and at the top of that column write "no". Then in the middle column, write "maybe," at the top.

When you've got those three columns created with yes to the left, maybe in the middle, no to the right, then go through and start to write some things in the yes column; things that you can immediately give a firm "yes" answer to. Things like "Will I always be there for my daughter? Yes!" With that one, there's nothing for me to think about. If my daughter needs me, my family needs me, yes, that's an immediate "yes", I know it, and it goes in that column.

Now, go to the "no" column. Here, you're going to write things, that as soon as they come up for consideration-boom- you can immediately say "no" to them.

In my "no" column, for example, stealing, would be there. Would I ever steal? No. Absolutely not. So I write stealing in that column.

Finally, go to the middle where you have your "maybe." Write down the things that are currently "maybe" in your life. Things that you're going to "get back to someone" about. Maybe a friend, a boss, your spouse, your children, things you're thinking about... that you said "maybe" to, when you were asked. I have down on my middle column, "buying more chickens." I have a few chickens here on the farm, most of them are hens, and they lay beautiful brown eggs. My daughter sells eggs to a few people, and when we really get eggs stacked up, we just give them away. I've been thinking about buying a few more chickens. So that's a "maybe" because I haven't bought them and I haven't said "no." So that's in the middle column. Going to the Amazon and taking a float down the Amazon River is also in my "maybe" column. I haven't called and booked the trip, and I haven't said "no" to the trip, it's a "maybe."

What's the point of all of this? Why take this out and create this sheet of three columns-yes, maybe, no? It's simple. You look at the middle column, the "maybe" column, and you make it your primary goal, to get everything out of the "maybe" column. It either goes to the "yes" column or it goes to the "no" column. The moment it has gone to either of those columns, you have cleared a massive amount of emotional and mental space, and you'll feel a huge sense of relief. You've made space for *other* things. The middle "maybe" row is clutter; mental clutter. It's taking up unnecessary space.

You might want to do this once a week, once a month, or once a quarter. You'll have to decide what's right for you. However, at the very least, from time to time, take out a piece of paper, make three columns, get very clear on your "yes", "no", and your "maybe" answers, and then work to clear out as many "maybe" answers as you can.

I promise you, when you are successful in clearing the "maybes" out of that middle column, and making them either a "no" or a "yes", you will live a more relaxed and more productive life.

Back to learning to say "no"

Stephen Covey, author of <u>Seven Habits of Highly Effective People</u> says that we can easily say "no" when we have a much bigger "yes" burning deep inside. For example, if I know that tomorrow night is my daughter's baseball game, from 6:30 to 7:30, it doesn't matter, at that point what somebody else comes up and asks me to do something. I'm not going to struggle with saying "no." That will be the easiest "no" I've ever said in my life. Someone might ask "Hey would you like to do this? It's a very important cause." "No, I'm busy tomorrow night at that time." It's so simple and so easy. Why is it so simple? Why does it just roll of the tongue like that with confidence, but a relaxed confidence? It's so easy, because I had a much bigger "yes" burning deep inside.

If you find that you've been having trouble saying "no" to the requests of others, it might not necessarily be that you don't have a bigger "YES", it might simply be that you're not aware of your bigger "YES." All you need to do is shift your awareness, and become aware of the big "YESES" in your life.

The moment you realize what the big "YESES" are in your life, when people are asking you to do things that are in conflict with those big "YESES" in your life, you'll have no trouble at all; you'll gladly and comfortably say "No, I can't. Maybe some other time" and that's that.

When you do say "no", don't embarrass yourself and lower your self-worth in the eyes of others, by apologizing. I often hear people make a slobbering apology; this longwinded list of reasons and excuses of why they can't...after they have said "no."There's really nothing that sounds any more pathetic and weak than that. And that's not the position you want to take, or it's certainly not the reputation you want to develop in business, or anywhere in life, of thinking that you have to justify it every time you say "no" to someone.

I don't justify; if I can't do it, if I don't want to do it, I'm simply going to say, "No, but thank you for asking." And that's it.

Never in my life, have I ever had somebody say, "Well, wait a minute, you didn't give me a list of five good reasons why you're not going to." People don't do that.

What people will do, most often, in response to your "no", is ask, "Are you sure? I'd really like you to think this over because we really think you'll be good for this." When this happens, I don't start providing a list of reasons. Instead, I just simply re-state, "No. I'm not interested. But thank you for asking." If I'm asked 5 times in a row, I will simply restate my previous answer 5 times in a row.

Learn to say "no." You'll be able to say "no" easily and effort-lessly when you learn what your big "YESES" are and make them crystal clear in your mind.

Strategy # 20:

Eat a Light Lunch

---

*"Ask not what can you do for your country;
ask what's for lunch"*
-ORSON WELLS

Most people either eat too much or they eat the wrong kinds of foods for lunch, and as a result what happens between 1 and 2 o clock pm., is that they experience what is known as the "midday slump." Most people think of the midday slump as this human condition that all humans *must* experience and that you can't escape because it's genetic.

Nothing could be further from the truth, because as you start to experiment with this and find out what foods work best for you, and start to reduce the amount of food that you're eating at lunch, you're going to find that you can reduce your experience of the midday slump. You're also going to find that once you've really targeted in on the food that is right for you, and the amount that is appropriate for you, you're going to find that you can *completely bypass* the midday slump.

If you're really tuned into this-once you find the food that nourishes you and energizes you, and eat just the right amount of it, you're going to find that lunch can have the opposite effect for you. You're going to find that eating the right kind of lunch and the right amount, is going to take you in the other direction, and it's going to take you and your energy level up a notch. How would that be? How would that be to experience a lunch where 30 minutes to an hour later you actually have *more* energy than you had before lunch?

That's a foreign concept to some people. Some people just can't fathom having *more* energy after lunch; it's amazing. Everybody knows what eating too much will do to you. Isn't that right? Everybody knows, and can remember it, and think about the last Thanksgiving dinner, or the big Christmas dinner, or just a big meal, period. You don't have to guess what that experience will be like. You know from previous experience if you eat too much of anything you're going to be tired, and you're going to have a hard time keeping your eyes open.

That's not what you want. You want more energy. You want to feel lighter in a sense, even though you've just eaten something. You want to feel your eyes open wider and a little more pep in our step. You want to feel invigorated from your lunchtime meal. And you might be asking "Is that possible?" Yes, it's possible.

We're not going to be delving too deep into the science of this, just remember that it all comes down to keeping your blood glucose, or "blood sugar" in a nice, tight range. If you were to graph your blood sugar over the course of a day, ideally what you'd like to see is a line that goes straight across with just a few wiggles in it. Unfortunately, if most people were to graph their blood sugar levels, taking them once an hour throughout the day, most adults would see something that looks like the Richter scale reading during an earthquake.

They would see these big peaks and then these deep troughs. That's not healthy in any sense. That's not healthy for you physically, mentally or emotionally. In fact, it undermines your health, whether you have diabetes or heart disease in your family or not.

Research is showing that so many of the habits people have today are able to bypass the genetic predisposition they may have for a particular disease, and somehow bring it about anyway. The predisposition for diabetes (or many other illnesses) doesn't necessarily need to be there in our family for the illness to surface.

But we're looking at productivity, right? We are focused on right now. How can I get more out of myself? How can I get more out of myself today, tomorrow, right now? And the quickest way from a physical energy level, is to eat less. Have a salad or vegetables for lunch. The nice thing about a salad and vegetables are most vegetables are very low in carbohydrates. If you eat a salad or plate of steamed or raw vegetables, not only are you *not* going to feel that crash, but you're going to be providing your body with just enough nutrition to bring your blood sugar levels up to where they need to be, and then stabilize them until your next snack or meal.

Let's say your typical afternoon slump lasts for an hour. How effective are you during that slump? How effective are you at focusing? How effective are you at catching the mistakes of other people on critical projects? How effective are you at noticing your own mistakes? How creative are you in this hour during your afternoon slump?

The bottom line is this: we both know that when we eat too much and when we use food that causes us to go down in energy, rather than go up with a little bit more energy, we know that our effectiveness drops dramatically.

We can bypass the energy slump by eating less; by eating vegetables; eating a salad, having a glass of tea, having a glass of water, staying away from the sugary drinks, staying away from the soft drinks, staying away from the sweetened tea.

And I know some people reading this will say, "Oh, the sweet tea! But you don't get it Vince, I'm from the Deep South and we're raised on sweet tea, I mean they don't put milk in our bottles when we're babies, they put sweet tea in our bottles." That may be. And it's also true that dumping sugar into your body and spiking your blood sugar rapidly causes your blood sugar to crash just as rapidly as it shot up, and you get this constant cycle where we need to bring our blood sugar back up.

When you bring it back up with the same foods and drinks that shot it up high and fast in the first place, it simply crashes down again. In the long term it literally undermines your health and leads you to an early grave.

When this cycle is happening, in the short term we're not nearly as effective. We don't get nearly as much done. We're not as good of a parent, teacher, spouse, supervisor, manager, CEO, whatever it may be. If you will start eating less at lunch, and eliminate as many if not all of the carbs-such as potatoes, rice, breads, sweets, soft drinks etc.-you will notice that you have more physical energy, and mental clarity.

If you will do that for a week I guarantee you there will be no turning back, because once you've felt it 2 days back to back, and you skip completely over that old afternoon slump and you actually feel like doing something after work, you're going to be hooked. Furthermore, you're going to enjoy not going through the old experience of "Oh, I'm tired, it was a hard day at work." each evening.

You're now saying "You know, it's strange. It was kind of a hard day at work, but I have a lot of energy tonight." One of the primary reasons for that will be you've decreased the load on your body. You're not requiring it to grind out as much of your physical energy to digest your food. Make it easier on your stomach, and I promise you, your stomach will make it easier on you.

Strategy # 21:

Estimate the Time
and Add 50 %

"In preparing for battle I have always found that plans are use-less, but planning is indispensable"
-DWIGHT D. EISENHOWER

It was once said that we overestimate what we can do in a week and underestimate what we can do in 10 years. I know I've found that to be true in my life, as I look back, and I'm sure you can too. We tend to look at the things on our list, or the things we have to do today, and as we put those things on our mental "to do" list, we estimate how long it's going to take. As you have probably experienced, we usually are wrong.

We guess something will take 30 minutes, "Oh I can whip that out real quick, I can do that in 30 minutes" , and so we allot, in our mind, about 30 minutes for that task, and we do that for each thing on our list. We look at our schedules and lists, and because we have underestimated how long something's going to take, we wind up putting more things on our schedule or our list than we can actually get to; but something more important happens here.

When we underestimate how long something is going to take, and we estimate 30 minutes that we thought this task would take, and we experience one mini-failure after another throughout the day-in terms of things we're not able to accomplish in the timeframe we thought-our momentum comes to a halt.

I'm sure you've experienced the other side of this as well; maybe you've estimated that something was going to take 2 hours, and you actually got it done in an hour. You know how good that feels. You feel lighter and you feel more motivated to take the next action.

Well, if you want to experience that more often, and you want to lower your stress level, there are certain things you have to do. One of the most effective methods you can use to do this, is to estimate how long something is going to take you and add 50 % to that.

For example, if you estimate that something is going to take you 30 minutes, add 50 % to that. It's going to take 45 minutes now. If you estimate that something is going to take an hour, you add 50 % to that, you've now got an hour and a half. If it's 2 hours, add 50 %, you've now got 3 hours.

A lot of the time, even though we might initially think of it as an extra 50 % cushion, in truth we're just giving ourselves the time we actually need to get the task done. However, at other times, you're going to have the experience of getting done early, and using this method you're going to get done early far more often than you're going to finish something late, or not on time. It comes back to that mental and emotional state and that feeling of accomplishment.

I used that term "mini-failures" earlier; because any time we plant the seed in our mind of how long something should take, or how far we should be able to get through something-whatever it is we're using as a standard of measurement- once we have fixed that in our mind, when we fall short, we're going to experience a mental and emotional letdown; a letdown is a form of stress and when our stress level goes up, our productivity level goes down.

So this is taking us in another direction. We are actually going to be getting things done on time or ahead of time. On time is adequate, ahead of time is great. It's when we hit the time limit we had fixed in our mind, and we're still not done, that our productivity goes down.

Use this method of adding 50% to the estimated time and keep your mental and emotional status on track.

Strategy # 22:

Let People Know Upfront How Much

Time You Have

"Say no to everything, so you can say yes to the one thing"
-RICHIE NORTON

Let people know upfront how much time you have. Let's say that somebody knocks on your office door and they say, "I've got something really important I need to talk to you about. Can I come in? I just need a few minutes." The tendency is to do one of two things. Say "No, I can't right now, now's not a good time," or simply "Okay yeah, come on in." I don't think I have to tell you that of the two, the thing people say more often is "Yes, come on in." Some people have a very difficult time saying "no", so they wind up saying "yes" when what they really should say is "no."

But for this example, let's talk about when people say "yes." When we say something as ambiguous as "yes, come on in" we have by, implication, told the other person that we have as much time as they need to discuss whatever it is they came in to discuss. When people come into your office and sit down in a nice overstuffed leather chair, they can take something that would take really only 5 minutes to discuss and outline, and expand that into 15, 20, or 30 minutes.

The challenge is, especially if you're the type of person who has a hard time saying "no", how likely do you think it is that you're going to be able to say "no", or shut them off after they've already come in? That's probably not going to happen. You solve this problem by letting them know, in the very beginning, exactly how much time you have. Set the frame of reference of how much time you have for them, and therefore, how much time they have to effectively communicate their needs, concerns, or to ask whatever question it is they have to ask you.

When you do this, something almost magical happens. If you tell someone that you only have 5 minutes, in most cases, even if they had something that would take 10-15 minutes in normal circumstances, once you have placed a frame of reference on the time available for both them and for you, their mind will be doing an instant editing job. It will start cutting out all the extemporaneous nonsense that really should have been cut out in the first place and they will narrow it down as closely as they can to only the content that actually needs to be discussed, or the only questions that need to be asked.

This works both ways. People can come in with something that would normally take 5 minutes and expand it into an hour if they're given that hour, or people could come in with something that would take an hour and contract it and condense it and refine it down to 10, 15, 20 minutes. They'll only do that when they are given a reason to do so. The reason is that you are only providing them with a finite and definite amount of time.

It would go something like this: they would say, "I've got something I've really been needing to ask you," or "I need to talk about this particular project. Do you have time to talk to me?" Instead of saying "Sure, come on in," you would say "Sure, but I only have five minutes. Can you do what you need to do in 5 minutes?" or "Sure, I need to tell you, though, I only have 15 minutes, and 15 minutes only, can you do what you need to do in 15 minutes?" When you do that, you will have placed a frame of reference around it. They will condense it, not expand it. This will make it much easier for you to get on with your day.

If you tell someone you only have 5 minutes, stick to it. Don't go over it by one minute, because we often complain about how other people treat or interact with us, but one thing we don't like to face that's so often true, is that we train other people how to treat us; we teach them how we will allow them to treat us.

If I tell somebody I only have 5 minutes, and they're leaving my office 20 minutes later, I am, by my own behaviors, training them to know that I don't mean what I say, and I don't say what I mean. So if you tell someone you only have 5 minutes, stick to 5 minutes, and you can do that initially, in very subtle ways. When it's approaching the 5 minute mark, glance down at your watch. That's a very powerful nonverbal cue that lets the other person know they should check their watch, and that you're aware of the fact that you told them you only have 5 minutes.

If that doesn't get it, you might glance down at your watch, notice their response, and if they don't have much of a response, then go ahead and just push away from your desk and stand up. Obviously, I'm using this in an office setting. I know you're an intelligent enough man or woman to be able to take this concept and apply this at home. Apply it, use it, and enjoy finding yourself getting more accomplished in your life.

Strategy #23:

Don't Live by Assumptions; Operate on Facts

"It is tempting, if the only tool you have is a hammer, to treat everything as if it were a nail"

–ABRAHAM MASLOW

When we make assumptions, we are drawing conclusions with partial information. If we assume that out favorite restaurant has a 25% discount on the steak dinner on Friday evenings, and order the steak based on that assumption, without verifying it with the waitress, we wind up paying 25% more than we had planned. This is not exactly earth shattering. However, when we make assumptions about things that have to do with our health and well-being, our faulty conclusion has the potential to cost us our life.

I conduct a seminar called The Psychology of Violence. In this seminar, I peel back the many layers on the inner workings of the minds of violent criminals, and teach seminar participants how the mental and emotional states they experience during an encounter with a violent criminal will have as much to do with their survival as anything else.

One demonstration I do that always leaves people dumbfounded is what I call the "Death is Closer than You Think" exercise. I start by asking this question, "If you had a loaded handgun tucked in your belt, or in a concealed holster, and saw a man with a knife off in the distance, angrily approaching, but then he stopped 21 feet from you, and just stood there staring at you, would you feel that you are in a decent position to defend yourself, in the event he should make a move towards you?"

My experience has been that almost everyone gives me some version of, "Oh, well yes, if I have a gun, and he is 21 feet away from me, if he decides to come at me with his knife, to either injure or kill me, I'll just blow him away!"

The factor that causes them to have the false sense of security, isn't what you think. It is not the gun. It's the 21 feet between them and the man with the knife. It's a distance that they feel will allow them more than enough time to pull their weapon and shoot the attacker before he reaches them. This assumption, as they are about to discover, would have gotten them killed.

I show them an exercise that was developed by a Salt Lake City, Utah police officer, who had been tasked with instructing junior officers on when to shoot, or not shoot, when facing someone who was wielding a knife, club, hatchet or similar weapon. When he started to put the training together, he quickly found there was no data available-anywhere-on what distance was safe, and what distance was not. He started doing his own experiments, as he knew what he would be teaching his fellow police officers would have to be accurate, or he might be handing them a death sentence.

As it turns out, the distance required to have ample time to draw a weapon and shoot an attacker who had decided to charge you with a knife, hatchet or other similar weapon, was much further than anyone might have imagined. The distance from which an attacker could charge and successfully stab a police officer before he could draw his weapon and fire, was much shorter than anyone might have imagined.

In my seminars, I ask for one of the more youthful and able bodied participants to come to the front of the room. I give them a non-operational handgun that is for training exercises. It is plastic, but the same size and weight as a real handgun. I ask them to place it inside their pants, like tucked into the small of their back, underneath their belt.

Then, I walk to a spot 21 feet away-directly across from them and turn to face them. I have a rubber training "knife", with blue chalk placed on the blade. I give them the following instructions, "In just a moment, I am going to suddenly and quickly charge at you with this knife. My intention is to contact you with the knife somewhere on your body that would represent a potentially lethal stab or slash. What I want you to do, the moment you see me start my charge, is pull your weapon, and bring it up in a manner that would allow you enough control to accurately place a stopping shot somewhere in my body."

After asking if they have any questions, I say, "Okay, be ready; it's coming anytime, you just don't know when." After pausing a few more seconds, I suddenly charge across the floor towards them, with my "knife" at the ready. I have done this demonstration dozens of times. I have done it with professional boxers who have lightning fast hand speed, people who have been carrying and shooting handguns for years, and I have done it with those who have been in law enforcement for a lengthy period of time.

One thing is the same, no matter who I do this with; I always close the gap and deliver at least one potentially lethal stab or slash-oftentimes more than one- before they can draw their weapon and bring it up in a way that would allow for a likely stopping shot. Most of the time, they don't even have the weapon pulled completely before I have "stabbed or slashed" them.

Clearly, 21 feet isn't enough, and 30 feet isn't all that much better, in terms of how many people can effectively draw their weapon and accurately fire. (However, any added distance is better than nothing.)

If you thought the purpose of this article was to focus on what distance you should have between you and your potential attacker when you draw your weapon, then I'm going to surprise you. I just wanted to give a very vivid example of where making a faulty assumption could cost someone their life.

Here's another faulty assumption people make—one about how knife attacks occur in the first place. In the real world, the world that does not happen in training rooms during seminars, those who attack someone with a knife, usually don't pull the knife and show it to the person they intend to stab or cut, before they attack. FBI statistics on this type of crime show a very different picture than the one we usually see depicted on screen by Hollywood producers. What happens is nearly impossible to defend against. In fact, the only reliable way to "defend" against this kind of knife attack is to simply not be there, period.

In one documented case after another, the first glimpse of a knife the victim sees-if they ever see it-is milliseconds before it is plunged into their chest, face, or abdomen. In a large percentage of these documented cases, the first stab or slash is a lethal strike. In short, knife attackers who truly have the intent of killing you, utilize the element of surprise. They keep the knife concealed as they close the distance, getting as close to you as possible, and then, when they are within striking distance, savagely stab or slash you repeatedly.

If you think there is anyone on the planet, or that there has ever been anyone on the planet, that has some "mystical" ability to defend against this kind of attack, I would argue that you have allowed Hollywood to shape your sense of reality about violence. There is not now, nor has there ever been anyone, or any method, that can reliably defend against an up close surprise attack with a knife. In movies, knives are shown to the person who will be stabbed, before they are stabbed, not because it reflects reality; but because it generates tension in movie goers that producers want to create. It's as simple as that.

Let's look at what this has to do with increasing your ability to get things done. I've used knife attacks as an example that has a much nastier consequence for making a faulty assumption than the consequences for most faulty assumptions you are likely to make during the course of your work day. I did that for a very important reason. Because of the vivid and emotional states an example like that elicits, you are far more likely to remember this topic and have a clear and concise reference for applying it elsewhere in your life.

If you take the time to think back on some of the recurring

moments of frustration you've had during the last 12 months, you'll likely find that at least some of them continue to be experienced because of some type of erroneous assumption you have been using. Perhaps it was an assumption about someone else, an assumption about the policy or procedures someone else or a business uses, or it might even have been an assumption about yourself, and what you would or wouldn't do.

Whatever it might be, when the event that triggered your frustration ensued, if you are like many other people, you didn't question the assumptions you had made that lead to what just happened. Instead, you may have simply channeled your frustration into vehemently demanding that "something" needs to change, and focus on what needs to happen "out there" so that you will never again experience the frustration you just did.

For example, let's look at the sales manager who, once again, is close to pulling their hair out after looking at yet another weekly sales report on the sales of one of their salesmen or saleswomen, who simply aren't producing at an acceptable level. In each private meeting the sales manager has with the struggling person, the salesperson nods and says, "Yes, I agree, I will start doing the things you have suggested and get my sales up!" to all of the suggestions expressed by the sales manager. After each meeting, the sales manager feels a renewed sense of hope, and is excited to see how much sales will increase in the coming weeks, but the increase in sales never comes to fruition.

How does this happen? It happens, largely because of a faulty assumption that goes like this, "I believe this salesperson will change. I believe they will increase their sales. All they need is some further training and some motivation. I will provide both, and we'll get this going!"

Having a belief like this is optimistic and fosters the kind of attitude that is central to being able to develop a crack sales team. However, once feedback has been produced, and the feedback continues on the same track, week after week, that indicates someone is not producing, and is not changing, it's time to step back and question what our assumptions about the situation might be.

Failing to periodically examine our assumptions and beliefs all but guarantees that we will often be acting and making decisions based on information that simply is not true.

The fact is, a sales manager has one primary job: to produce as many sales as possible. The time the sales manager has available is limited. Time frittered away with someone that the available feedback indicates is not going to become someone who will produce the quota, is time that is no longer available for recruiting someone else who will, or time that can be used to enhance the sales of the people who are *already* considered "producers".

The most likely reason a sales manager will continue, week after week, though, is the faulty assumption that ignores all feedback to the contrary. The assumption of, "I believe this salesperson will change. I believe they will increase their sales. All they need is some further training, and some motivation. I will provide both, and we'll get this going!"

As you begin examining your own assumptions, you'll be surprised, maybe even shocked, at how many of them are based on very little evidence that supports the validity of a given assumption. You may even find assumptions that are built on no evidence and are little more than cute little anecdotes that had been passed down to you by well-meaning parents, or that you had vicariously picked up while on your journey through life.

What do you need to do with your faulty assumptions once they've been discovered? Not much, really. The power of the "spotlight" of awareness is very often enough to dismantle the faulty assumption, and break the hold it has had in how you process the world around you.

How can that be? When you first learned there was no Santa Claus or Easter Bunny, did you need to attend workshops on changing and updating your beliefs? Did you require therapy to deal with the fact that for years, you have behaved the way you did around Christmas, based on something that wasn't really true? Of course not. The moment you realized that you were now in possession of more accurate information, your behaviors and feelings naturally aligned with your newly discovered reality, and that was that.

You'll find the same to be true with how it works when you uncover faulty assumptions. The old way of thinking and behaving will fall away and be replaced with the kinds of thoughts and behaviors that are the best fit for your new, and more updated and accurate assumptions and beliefs.

Here are a few questions you can ask about any given belief or assumption to determine how valid it is, and whether it is serving you in a useful way:

1.   Ask "How do I know this is true?" This will force you to examine what "proof" you have to support this belief. I will tell you ahead of time, when you ask this question, be prepared to be

shocked at just how little "proof" you have for many of the beliefs you use to guide your behavior.

2.   Ask "Is this assumption or belief one that I would want to pass on to my children? Is it one I would want them using as a guidepost for their own thinking, feeling and behaving as they move through the world?" The beliefs and assumptions we are quick to defend, can often destabilize a bit when you view them as ideas that would impact and influence those you love most

3.   Ask "Where did I learn this way of thinking? Who taught me this, or where did I pick it up?" This does something that is very powerful. It gets us to notice something that we have most likely forgotten; the fact that we weren't born with this assumption or belief and that at some point we went from not thinking that way, to thinking that way, and it came about as a result of something we learned from someone else. Which leads to the next question.

4.   Ask "How does that person know this is true?" Once you've identified where you learned this assumption or belief, you can apply a question that is similar to the one suggested above. Again, I caution you. Be prepared to discover how many times you come to realize that the person who shared the assumption or belief with you, either directly, or indirectly, doesn't really have much valid evidence that the assumption is true.

With these four questions, and the awareness to start noticing and spotting your beliefs and assumptions, you will be able to literally begin altering the way you process life, the world around you, and be able to experience life in a more enjoyable way, while getting more done and becoming more productive.

Strategy #24:

The Mouse Exercise

"You know you're in love when you can't fall asleep because reality is finally better than your dreams"
-DR. SEUSS

Want an exercise that will demonstrate that we, as human beings, create most of our experience of the world on the inside, and then project it to the outside world, and act as thought what we created, is real?

This will require you to actually take a few moments and STOP and DO the following exercise, or it won't be effective.

Imagine a mouse on the floor about 5-8 feet in front of you. Actually stop, look away from the pages of this book and do this. See it there, imagine it in great detail. Notice every detail about this mouse that you can. Do this, now, so you can experience something really profound in just a moment.

Now, if you actually stopped to do the exercise (if you didn't, please stop now, and go back and do so, before reading on) I have some questions for you. Take a moment to stop and think about the answers to each question before going to the next question.

About how long was the mouse's tail?

How big were his ears compared to a hamsters ears?

Was his fur darker towards the front of his body, or the back?

Were the pink pads of his feet visible?

Assuming you actually did the first part of this, and took the time to think about and answer my questions that followed, I know something very specific about you.

When you thought about the answer to each question like "Are the pink pads of his feet visible?" you actually looked back at the place where you "saw" the mouse I asked you to imagine.

You looked back where you had imagined a mouse, but where you KNEW there was no actual mouse. Because once we imagine something vividly enough, we automatically project it to the outside world, and interact with it like it REALLY IS out "there", even though it is not.

This exercise reflects a great deal about the beauty of our imagination and how many people unknowingly use their own brain to create a world of problems that don't really exist except in their own mind.

Consider the following questions:

1.   How many of the things you've been worrying about, most recently, have actually existed for you to see?

2.   How many of the things you've been worrying about, most recently, have existed primarily inside the "theater" of your own mind and imagination?

3.   How many of the things you've been worrying about,

most recently, whether they exist in the real, external world, or not, have been made worse, by the images you've created in the "theater" of your own mind and imagination?

4.   How much have you hurt your productivity and your ability to take action by the images you've created in the "theater" of your own mind and imagination, and by treating them as real?

5.   How much could you boost your productivity and motivation to take action, by taking conscious control of the images you've created in the "theater" of your own mind and imagination?

6.   When will you begin to take control of the images you've created in the "theater" of your own mind and imagination?

Walt Disney had his life changed by a mouse. While you may not desire your own Disney Land, you, too, can let a mouse change your life. Reflect back on the mouse exercise from time to time, as a reminder of just how prone we are to take the images in our mind-the ones we create-and then project them outwardly, treating them as "real."

Strategy # 25:

Why Affirmations Rarely Work and Can Even Make Matters Worse
(and what you can do about it)

"Perseverance is failing 19 times and succeeding the 20th."

-JULIE ANDREWS

Many of my clients over the years have become my clients because of some form of internal conflict they have been experiencing. For example, maybe someone who is a few pounds overweight experiences the ongoing inner conflict of one thought saying, "You better not eat that! You know you need to lose weight and that will make you even fatter!" and another saying, "You only have one life to live, so you better enjoy it; go ahead... eat it and enjoy life!" This sets up a mental and emotional form of self-torture.

Many books, therapists, counselors etc. suggest to their clients that they change their self image by saying positive affirmations to themselves. While the intention is usually good, because so few people truly understand how the human brain processes language, and how that processing impacts people on an emotional level, most give instructions for doing affirmations that lead to disastrous results.

First, to truly understand what happens, we need to understand something about the people experiencing this internal conflict. When people don't like something about themselves, they tend to reject or criticize themselves. This is the exact opposite of self-acceptance.

Therefore, when they are taught about affirmations, they are usually taught to first begin with statements about accepting themselves. Statements like, "I deeply and fully accept myself", and this is where the trouble begins.

A statement like that creates major conflict between the rejection and criticism of themselves that was already going on, and the new statement of self-acceptance. Naturally, the unconscious mind rejects the self-acceptance statement, no matter how many times it is repeated, because of the direct conflict between the two opposing ideas.

Furthermore, because the unconscious doesn't believe the self-acceptance statement, the more it is repeated, the more it doesn't believe it, and the person begins to feel more and more like a "fraud", and this opens up a very profound "can of worms", emotionally.

Fortunately, there is a rather straight forward way around this linguistic nightmare.

Think of something you might sometimes say to yourself that you don't like. For example, some of my clients had said, "I'm just a fat pig, so I'll never lose weight"

Whatever your statement is, say your negative statement to yourself. Then, after you have, try saying, "I completely and fully accept myself."

How much did you feel like you accepted the "acceptance" comment? For most people, they tell me, "Not at all!" Now, I'm going to have you add two simple words: "Even though"

Take your negative statement, such as "I'm just a fat pig..." and put "Even though" in front of it. So, it becomes, "Even though I'm a fat pig..." and then add a positive statement to the end, like "...I can learn to lose weight." It becomes, "Even though I'm a fat pig, I can learn to lose weight."

Why does this suddenly become believable? It's simple, really; the words "even though" have an interesting way of neurologically linking the contradictory statements. You are no longer denying the idea you had already believed (that you are a fat pig) so you're no longer triggering internal unconscious resistance, and because you aren't, your mind is far more accepting of suggestions that will offer a way out of being a "fat pig."

I could write for days on this topic alone, and still not cover it all. However, I would only succeed in creating confusion about what is really an amazingly embarrassingly simple concept. You have before you, the raw materials for transforming some of your internal conflict, far more easily than you might have previously thought. Two words, "Even though..." can take things that have been difficult, and that caused you to self-sabotage, and create an inner environment of harmony and ease. Let it, and it will.

About the Author

Vincent Harris is a renowned Peak Performance coach and the bestselling author of <u>The Productivity Epiphany, and Bypassing No in Business.</u> He has spent 15 years as a coach, adviser and consultant for men and women from all over the world, having earned the nickname, "The Human Whisperer" from one of the many psychologists who routinely call Vince for help with their difficult clients or patients. He has the ability to see things, where others don't, and the ability to do things, that others can't... or just won't. In the end, though, no matter what approach he takes, Vince's clients change, and their lives become more productive and enjoyable.